POINT CONCEPTION TO MEXICO

A COMMON MAN KAYAK ADVENTURE

DANA,

IT'S RATHER LIGHT READING,
BUT I HOPE YOU ENJOY IT.

POINT CONCEPTION TO MEXICO

A COMMON MAN KAYAK ADVENTURE

David Powdrell

Illustrated by Peggy Lindt

First Edition

Cuatro Casas Company Publishing
Santa Barbara, California

POINT CONCEPTION TO MEXICO
A COMMON MAN KAYAK ADVENTURE

By David Powdrell
Published by: Cuatro Casas Company Publishing
                   5290 Overpass Road, Suite 227
                   Santa Barbara, California 93111 USA

Library of Congress Cataloging-in-Publication Data
Powdrell, David
     Point Conception to Mexico: A Common Man Kayak Adventure / by David Powdrell. – 1st ed.
   p. cm. Includes bibliographical references.

   Kayaking – United States. I. Title
   Camping – Southern California
   Travel – California coastline

Library of Congress Card Number: 98-92654   CIP

ISBN 0-9663634-0-X

TABLE OF CONTENTS

PREFACE

A
s I sit at my computer entering my journal, I am quick to learn that there are caveats that the reader should be aware of.

First, I am an accountant by trade, not a professional writer, two careers that are on opposite sides of the creativity spectrum. I love reading, but rarely take up a pen to write anything other than Christmas cards and responses to Internal Revenue Service queries on behalf of my clients. As a CPA with a master's degree in taxation, I am somewhat comfortable with tax law. I understand the logic behind why 7.5% of line 2 on Schedule A should be less than line 32 of Form 1040. Perhaps when all is said and done, I will look back and remind myself to stick to those things that I know, and let the wordsmiths of the world tell the stories. On the other hand, this has been an excellent adventure, a somewhat unique feat, and I'd like to tell the story in my own words.

Secondly, this is not a technical manual on kayaking. None of us are experts in kayaking. In fact, most of us were complete novices when we started this adventure. The major bookstores, however, have a large selection of kayak manuals and I would strongly recommend reading them to learn the basics of kayaking and to familiarize yourself with safety issues of kayaking before attempting any serious kayak camping adventures.

This journal, on the other hand, is a collection of memories with my best friends kayaking, surfing, and doing some of the silly things that grown men do while we camped and paddled the lower third of the State of California.

ACKNOWLEDGMENTS

Thanks go to the families of the guys that took part in this journey. It's generally a hardship, and perhaps sometimes a blessing, having these husbands and dads away from the household for several days at a time, but we all appreciate the chance to get together and pal around on our adventures.

Thanks also go to the following individuals who helped me put this journal together from scrap paper to final publication.

Derek Levy was an inspiration from the start. Throughout the process of editing and revising, he constantly kept his hand on the pulse and helped shape it to its final state. This journal would not be complete without his help.

Michael Tompane and Wendy Roth encouraged me through the difficult early stages. Thank you for that.

Thanks to Mark, Debbie, and Scott of PaddleSports of Santa Barbara for their patience while I constantly badgered them for advice, recommendations, books, videos, and discounts on kayak rentals.

My friends and critics reviewed the early editions of the manuscript giving me excellent recommendations. They include Lin Rolens, Autumn Steuchrath and Basil Honikman.

Peggy Lindt prepared the beautiful illustrations for the book. She captured the moments quite accurately when my camera wasn't accessible.

Martha Whitt is the professional proofreader who was absolutely invaluable. Her 7.3 million "author queries" were tactfully made, protecting my feelings while still getting the job done.

And finally, a hugh thank you to Kathleen Baushke for design, layout, and generally taking this complete novice through the steps of putting a book into publication. I was wandering aimlessly in the publication arena until she got involved. She is truly an expert in her field.

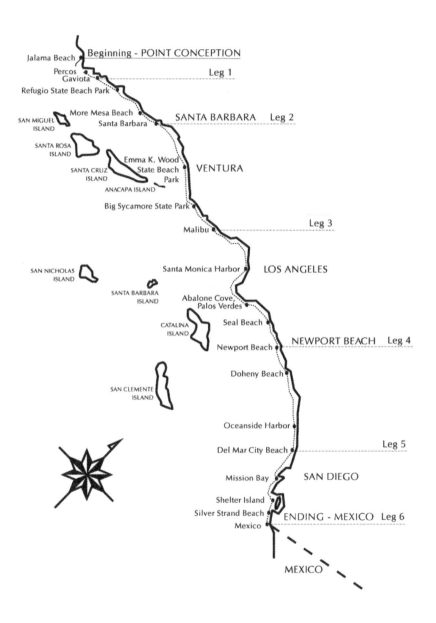

Beginning - POINT CONCEPTION

Jalama Beach

Percos

Gaviota   Leg 1

Refugio State Beach Park

More Mesa Beach   SANTA BARBARA   Leg 2

SAN MIGUEL

ISLAND   Santa Barbara

SANTA ROSA

ISLAND

Emma K. Wood   VENTURA

SANTA CRUZ   State Beach

ISLAND   Park

ANACAPA ISLAND

Big Sycamore State Park

Leg 3

Malibu

SAN NICHOLAS   Santa Monica Harbor   LOS ANGELES

ISLAND

SANTA BARBARA

ISLAND   Abalone Cove

Palos Verdes

CATALINA   Seal Beach

ISLAND   NEWPORT BEACH   Leg 4

Newport Beach

Doheny Beach

SAN CLEMENTE

ISLAND

Oceanside Harbor

Del Mar City Beach   Leg 5

Mission Bay   SAN DIEGO

Shelter Island

Silver Strand Beach   ENDING - MEXICO   Leg 6

Mexico

MEXICO

Each fully loaded Scupper Pro carried approximately 200 pounds of gear, including food, water, sleeping bags, and clothes.

The boys—Tim Ritter, Lee Walker, Derek Levy, Dave Powdrell, Mark Levy, Jim Doughty, John Beardsmore, Dave Baxter, and Doug Powdrell.

INTRODUCTION

THE MOTIVATION

N one of us are serious kayakers. Most of us are over 40 years old working through various mid-life crisis issues. We're plumbers, insurance brokers, accountants, and doctors. Most are married with adolescent children at home. Our journey from Point Conception to Mexico was intended to be a two-day, 25-mile kayaking and surfing trip from Jalama State Beach, around Point Conception, past the Bixby and Hollister Ranches to Gaviota State Beach. The trek grew into a second leg the following year from Gaviota to Santa Barbara. At the completion of Leg 2, we committed to make the full 344-mile journey to Mexico.

The initial idea was born after reading an article entitled "Surf Exploring Big Sur" by Jeff Chamberlain in the September 1994 issue of *Surfer's Journal*. Mr. Chamberlain details his experiences of exploring the rugged Northern California coastline by kayak and includes some breathtaking photography of remote beaches and surfing locations.

Another contributing factor is our love for surfing along the Hollister and Bixby Ranch shorelines, a remote 15-mile coastline an hour west of Santa Barbara. The surf along this coast is some of the best in California and because of its remoteness, is generally uncrowded.

We own a tiny, 13¹/₂ foot Boston Whaler, the *Semper Fi*, which we use to surf the Hollister and Bixby Ranches. Semper fi, meaning always faithful, is the U.S. Marine Corps motto. We named our little boat *Semper Fi* after a surfing expedition on the Camp Pendleton Marine Base a few years ago. Our little *Semper Fi* has a very temperamental motor, however, and is consistently unfaithful to us, which makes for an adventure every time we put out to sea. Fully rigged to carry six surfboards overhead and four people on board, it's a tight fit when the surf taxi is fully loaded.

The combination of Mr. Chamberlain's article and our surfing expeditions on the *Semper Fi* motivated us to take a stab at kayaking the first 25 miles of California coastline. Little did we know where it would eventually take us.

THE BOYS

Good friends, I've come to learn, are a gift. They should be treasured. Most guys, I believe, have a hard time admitting this, but I know that the group I traveled with feels this way. Diverse in their professions, family lives, and educational backgrounds, the common bond is our love of the ocean. We surf, kayak, dive, paddleboard, and fish as often as possible. We each have our particular strengths and weaknesses, but I trust these guys with my life.

Most of us have known each other for years; some of us have been friends since childhood days. For the past 15 years, we've taken dozens of surfing trips from as far south as Punta Baja on the coast of Baja, up to the frigid waters of San Simeon, California.

When together, we revert to 12-year-olds and laugh at most anything. It's a chance to let our guard down; nobody needs to be impressed. The word "knucklehead" comes up regularly when we're together and that's a good thing, in my opinion.

Five of us will do the entire journey from Jalama Beach to the Mexican border. We'll pick up other crew during various legs of the journey. In addition to kayaks, some will be on paddleboards. The primary characters of this adventure are:

Lee Walker of Manhattan Beach owns a successful insurance agency in downtown Los Angeles. Lee just turned 40 years old and is the most fit of all of us. He's got a full washboard stomach and is an athletic dynamo. I met Lee, an excellent snow skier, surfer, and volleyball player, while attending the University of Colorado at Boulder in 1974. We were best men at each other's wedding. If I were casting for a movie, Jean Claude Van Damme would play Lee Walker.

John Beardsmore is a plumbing contractor in Santa Barbara and an avid surfer. John will surf any size wave without fear and has this smooth graceful style about him, considering he's a lumbering 6'3" tall. John's also one of those people you love to have on camping trips; easygoing, great conversation, excellent sense of humor; nothing rattles him. If Dan Blocker of Bonanza fame were still alive, he'd play John Beardsmore in the movie.

Derek Levy operates the best chiropractic clinic in Manhattan Beach. Anyone who frequents 1st Street in Manhattan Beach knows Derek. An awesome surfer, Derek's also notoriously funny. He's sort of a walking comedy act, improvising as he strolls through life. Derek Levy is John Belushi reincarnated; Belushi would play Derek in my make-believe film.

Mark Levy, Derek's older brother, is also an expert surfer. Mark was the 1974 U.S. Surfing Champion. Now an expert paddleboarder, he's a world-class competitor in long-distance paddling. Mark and Derek recently set a world record time crossing the English Channel on their paddleboards. Mark is a part owner of a coffeehouse in Redondo Beach and has an engineering degree from the University of California at Berkeley. Because of his rugged good looks and Zen approach to paddling, my wife thinks Richard Gere should play Mark Levy, and I concur.

I'm an accountant, a squash player, surfer, former ski instructor, and generally a bit unorthodox. I recently overheard my seven-year-old daughter telling her friend "My Dad's weird," but that "it's a good kind of weird." My wife thinks Kevin Costner would play me in the movie (bless her), but the guys think Rick Moranis or Pat Sajak from "The Wheel of Fortune" are more fitting. Let's go with Costner.

My youngest brother, Doug Powdrell, is also an excellent big wave surfer. Having grown up in Palos Verdes, California, I have some wonderful memories of Doug casually gliding down 20-foot surf at Lunada Bay, California. Doug's the only one of us with extensive kayak experience, having done quite a bit of white water river kayaking near his home in Sacramento. He's also very entertaining on trips with his unique mannerisms and vision of the world. With college degrees in both marine biology and mechanical engineering, he works with the California Office of Emergency Services (OES) dealing with disasters throughout California. Perhaps 1960's surf icon Mickey Dora would come out of seclusion and play my brother in the movie.

Dave Baxter is an appraiser in Santa Barbara, an expert sailor, avid golfer, former beach volleyball standout, and the hit at any beach party. The license plate on his car reads LUNARK9 in respect to the *Beach Blanket Bingo* rascal of the 1950's, Moondoggie. Dave's usually got an ice cold home brew beer in one hand and is egging someone to get on their head and drink a beer. So it's only fitting that James Darrin, who played Moondoggie, play Dave Baxter in the movie.

Richard Herald, an engineer in Santa Barbara, joined us for the last 123 miles. An excellent conversationalist and athlete, Richard fit in beautifully with the group. Richard reminds me of a radio or TV personality with his crisp, clear dialect and impressive knowledge of the world. David "Cabin Boy" Letterman would make a cameo appearance as Richard Herald in the movie.

THE EQUIPMENT

The kayak that we will use on our journey is the Scupper Pro kayak made by Ocean Kayaks, Inc. These are the bright colored, plastic, sit-on-top kayaks you see at many beach resorts, but with hatches in the bow and stern for storing tents, sleeping bags, food and so forth. Just shy of 15 feet in length, they weigh 48 pounds empty, and approximately 250 pounds fully loaded. Significantly slower than virtually all enclosed kayaks, we generally do between three and five miles per hour, depending on current, wind, and fatigue. These kayaks cost around $900 new but can be found used in the classified ads for about half that much. They're also readily available for rent, which is important to us, as we own only three of these kayaks among all of us.

Scupper Pro kayaks don't have rudders, unlike most enclosed kayaks, so they're a bit harder to steer in cross currents and side angle waves. And, although the bow and stern hatches have rubber gaskets, water inevitably gets into the kayak.

Although these kayaks are known as the tricycles of the industry, we have a preference to them. Being rookie kayakers, none of us knows how to Eskimo roll an enclosed kayak, which might be required along this journey. The sit-on-top kayaks have storage capacity that is more than ample for our camping needs. And finally, these kayaks easily handle the abuse we subject them to around heavy surf and rocky cliffs.

The excellent staff at PaddleSports in Santa Barbara has been instrumental in providing kayaks to us for our adventures. Mark, Debbie and Scott have always been accommodating, inspirational, and a wealth of information to us neophytes.

LEG ONE

JALAMA BEACH TO GAVIOTA
NOVEMBER 4–5, 1994

CREW: Dave Powdrell, John Beardsmore, Lee Walker, Derek Levy, Doug Powdrell, and Erik Witthoft.

Packing for a kayak camping trip is not unlike most other camping trips except that you've got to assume that everything will slosh around in warm, solar-heated salt water inside the kayak hull. I've learned that paddling through surf, water inevitably seeps past the rubber gaskets into the hull. Everything that goes into the kayak is therefore wrapped up in one and sometimes two plastic trash bags. Our provisions include the bare essentials . . . food, water, a stove, sleeping bags, tents, dry clothes, duct tape, first aid kit, firewood, bocce balls, horse-shoes, tequila, cigars, plastic-coated playing cards, and our battery powered automatic card shuffler. Total weight is approximately 1,000 pounds of gear.

We carefully pack and repack the kayaks in my garage the night before the trip, and I'm sure that we're missing something. We'll be out two days on the open ocean with no access to the civilized world, which is the way all camping trips should be, in my opinion. We'll either improvise or do without when we discover what we forgot.

5:00 A.M. departure from Santa Barbara down the seemingly endless, winding road to Jalama Beach, the exterior air temperature reads a freezing 29 degrees from inside our warm, comfortable Dodge Caravan. As we step out of the van, the wind is blowing and the hair on my back stands to attention. The battle of stripping out of warm clothes and putting on a wetsuit is one that we've all done thousands of times when on surfing trips, but for some reason it feels different today. I suspect it's because we're going to places we've never been before, paddling distances not previously attempted, with no help within hours of our whereabouts, and in kayaks, not on our familiar surfboards.

The 58-degree water temperature feels like a bathtub relative to the frigid air temperature. The ocean is smooth and a beautiful deep blue. The skies are a softer watercolor blue and white, and the surrounding hillsides are lush green with long winter grass. Fortunately, the surf is mild, so we shouldn't get too wet going out. The surf at Jalama Beach can pound, especially this time of year, and I'm thankful that today the sets are only head high.

With surfboards towed behind the kayaks, we paddle out through the shorebreak. The waves demonstrate their strength by pulling two of the surfboards free from the towlines. After paddling back to shore, we reconfigure the method of transporting the surfboards by securing them with bungee cords directly onto the back of the kayak, fins up. This turns out to be the most efficient method of transporting surfboards as it also keeps the surfboard fins out of the many large kelp beds that we eventually encounter along the way.

With everyone somewhat settled in their kayaks, we begin the paddle toward Point Conception, a distant point five miles on the horizon. Within 15 minutes, we're just past Tarantulas, a popular surfing spot near Jalama State Park. With everyone in eyesight of each other, Derek points out something on the surface of the water. Some 50 yards ahead of us is a black fin, but not like the many dolphin fins we've seen while surfing. Dolphin fins come up to the surface, submerge, then rebound again in another place. This fin is moving slowly along the surface of the ocean looking much like the sail of a toy sailboat, and we are gaining on it. At closer view, I notice a second smaller fin trailing close behind the larger fin. Not having seen a shark on the ocean surface before, I'm guessing that it's a baby shark following its larger mother. Instead, the smaller fin turns out to be a tail fin behind the larger dorsal fin of a six-foot blue shark, gently gliding along the surface of the ocean. My stomach is uneasy as I quickly play out the various scenarios that could occur as we approach the shark. Best case: we paddle next to it and get the exhilaration of paddling with this magnificent creature in its natural habitat. Worst case: it's a great white shark on a feeding expedition, with many possibilities in between.

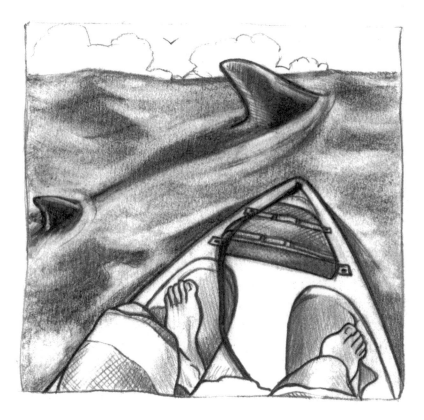

At about ten yards away, the shark senses our approach and instinctively submerges with a few swift thrusts of its tail. We conclude that the shark was out on leisurely sun basking swim, not the dreaded feeding excursion. We also conclude, given its color and size characteristics, that it's a blue shark, not the more dangerous great white, which makes me feel slightly better.

Nearing Point Conception, with the rest of the crew out of earshot, Derek and I see two much larger fins $^1/_4$ mile out to sea. I decide to get closer and paddle hard out to sea. As I'm approaching from behind, I assume the shark will quickly swim away, like the earlier shark. Instead, this larger shark gently continues to swim in front of me. I am gaining on it and am getting nervous. At about two feet behind it, I estimate that it's eight to ten feet in length. I can see the smooth water washing down its back as it glides on the ocean surface. Adrenaline is definitely flowing because I'm in its world, not SeaWorld, and I know that if it wants to, it can make my day miserable. Suddenly, the shark blasts off behind me with a few effortless thrusts! It circles me once before submerging to a greater depth. With the shark out of sight, I'm more nervous than when I was paddling next to it. I take a few more small, sheepish strokes with my paddle, wait patiently for a Jaws-like surprise lunge from the depths, then begin gingerly paddling back toward Derek.

It's awesome seeing any large beast of nature in its element. I am in awe of both the grace and speed of this blue shark as we approach Point Conception.

Having seen the shark up close is part of why I want to do this trip. I like to think of it as living life to its fullest and I'm always a strong supporter of that. I'm not certain how many people out of, say, ten would intentionally paddle out toward a shark in a kayak in the open ocean far from any help. My wife thinks less than five. I like to think more than eight.

We continue our paddle toward the lighthouse on Point Conception, an area known as Danger Area Nine on navigational maps. It is also the elbow of the state of California dividing Northern from Southern California, where vast quantities of water and air tend to move at fast and erratic rates.

We've had the pleasure to witness intense ocean conditions at Point Conception in the past. In early November 1992, we took the *Semper Fi* out to the Hollister Ranch for a surf trip. The following is a segment of an entry in my Hollister Ranch Surf Journal:

> Sunday, November 8, 1992: Crew: Derek Levy, Lee Walker, Todd Taugner, Dave Powdrell. Tides: Low 1:25 A.M. 1.6, High Tide 7:40 A.M. 5.7, Low Tide 2:34 P.M. 0.00. Water Temp: 63, Wind NW 10–15 knots, Marine Forecast: West Swell 3 foot, Point Conception Buoy: Seas 5 foot, Swell 10 foot, 13 second intervals. Small craft warning.
>
> Surfed Percos—7:30 A.M. to 3:00 P.M. Two- to four-foot surf. Fast inside wave at high tide. Completely different wave at low tide, mushier and breaking further out. West, around the bend at Point Conception for a quick look. We witness large, grinding swells. Unrideable. Dangerous. The angry dark ten-foot-plus swells dwarf the boat.

The swells and currents were completely different from those on the eastern side of the point. On that November day years ago, as we went around the Point Conception, we went from being a small, yet safe, watercraft to a totally vulnerable minnow, and I was scared. The dark gray swells tossed us around like a small toy in the bathtub and literally towered over us before crashing like thunder on the rock cliffs. There would be no way to get to shore at Point Conception if our typically unfaithful *Semper Fi* broke down. We'd have to swim out to open ocean, then hope that the swell and currents carried us southeast toward the Bixby Ranch beaches. If not, the pounding surf on the rock cliffs would most likely finish us off. Point Conception has been the demise of countless major ships and large boats. We didn't stay long in the tiny *Semper Fi*.

But today, on this crisp, clear November 4th, the swell is unusually mild, the wind has died completely and the ocean is sheet glass. There had been major storm warnings the week before, as there would be the following week. We are extremely fortunate to have entered a small window of opportunity at Point Conception in the wintertime. And it's sharing all its rugged beauty with us.

Derek and Doug unhook their surfboards and ride a small break among the rock outcrops in front of the lighthouse at Point

Conception. The 200-foot tall jagged sandstone cliffs that they surf toward are intimidating to me, but both confidently ride the waves. Very few people have ever surfed directly below the Point Conception lighthouse and few ever will.

Dozens of sea lions and harbor seals bark at us and splash us with their fins while Doug and Derek surf. I feel like the paperboy on a bicycle route while the neighborhood dogs chase and nip at my wheels, but the sea lions prove harmless. It tickles me how much the Pacific harbor seals look like my yellow labrador

retriever, Bartley, when he's chasing sticks in the surf, wet whiskers, slicked back hair, and big round dark eyes.

Continuing down the coast, we touch our oars to what we determine to be the apex of Point Conception, an unheard-of feat 360 days of the year, and perhaps a once-in-a-lifetime feat during winter months. Huge waves and howling winds pound these cliffs throughout most of the year, keeping mankind far from the Point Conception apex. We paddle into some dark rock amphitheaters along the cliffs, hooting and hollering. It is intimidating to snuggle up against these jagged, gnarly cliffs in tiny, fragile kayaks knowing that freighters and navy ships have been shipwrecked under 30-foot waves here. We're toying with Mother Nature, and she's patiently tolerating us.

About a mile east of Point Conception, we stumble upon a small crevice in the cliff walls. The opening is narrow and four of us decide, apprehensively, to paddle in. Not sure if it will narrow to a dead end, we gingerly continue down the dark rock corridor. Rather than narrowing, however, the opening continues to widen as we paddle. A group of California sea lions quickly surrounds us

in the water as we approach. The corridor eventually opens to a full 300-yard wide private beach with hundreds of Pacific harbor seals, California sea lions, and Northern elephant seals all barking, belching, and sun bathing. We have stumbled upon a major California seal rookery. The big male elephant seals, up to 21 feet long, and several of the smaller seals and sea lions waddle down off the beach and harass us with their barking and splashing. Their behavior continually becomes more aggressive as some of the seals are getting airborne within a few feet of us. Uneasy about this behavior, we take a few pictures before paddling back out to the open ocean.

After discussions with other more experienced kayakers and marine biologists back home, we learn that the rookery is the proverbial smorgasbord for great white sharks. The sharks swim down the small channel and circle around and around the small bay eating their fill of seal. Peter Howorth of the Marine Mammal Center in Santa Barbara informs me that there have been recent shark attacks in and near that rookery. Fortunately, we didn't add to that statistic.

Coming around Government Point we beeline it toward a familiar spot, Percos, located on the Bixby Ranch. A young Santa Barbara surfer/fisherman and his girlfriend chat with us for awhile before heading out to sea in their fishing boat, leaving Percos exclusively to us. Surfing some glassy 2'–4' waves under a fire red sunset, we're exhausted when we gather on the beach for cocktails and dinner.

Percos is a fantasy come true for me. Because of its topography, the sun both rises and sets over the ocean at Percos. The artist who paints the sky at Percos uses all the colors in his palette. The mix of those colors is like none I have encountered in my life.

When the waves are breaking at high tide at Percos, with nobody else in the water, I'm constantly pinching myself. A Percos wave allows even a novice surfer to look like a pro; an easy take-off and trim, the wave begins to bowl up and build on the inside section. The wave nearly doubles in size from the takeoff point and gets very hollow. The color of the water turns from a deep blue in the outer waters to translucent aqua marine on the shallow inside section. Derek and Mark have no trouble riding the tube sections for long periods when Percos is firing. In snow skiing terms, surfing at Percos is like skiing on Ruthie's Run at Aspen on a Wednesday afternoon with nobody else on the slope: pure bliss.

Camping out at Percos on the Bixby Ranch, however, is risky. Because it's private property, we're legally allowed to stay below the mean high tide line. That generally means in the wet sand.

But that also means that at 4:30 A.M. when the tide is highest, we will be sleeping in salt water.

Also, the missiles that launch from Vandenberg Air Force Base are aimed directly over the Bixby Ranch toward the Pacific Ocean. In the event of an errant misfire, the missiles either break up or are blown up, the fiery fragments falling to an open ocean. In September 1992, the U. S. government acquired the development rights to the Bixby Ranch by eminent domain for the sum of $22.1 million. In purchasing the building rights, the government's liability caused by misfires was significantly diminished. Although the Bixby heirs still own the land, only 38 homes can be built in designated areas, rather than the 490 homes, two golf courses, and equestrian center they had originally planned. Very few people will view this most beautiful property for generations to come.

Pulling the deadweight kayaks in close to the cliffs, we accumulate driftwood, set up camp, and make ourselves as inconspicuous as possible, like hiding six elephants on a dance floor. The worst case at this point is that the Bixby Ranch guard drives down in his white pickup truck and tells us we have to leave. The closest place to go would be back to Jalama State Park, some 9 miles west. Another option would be to paddle east 16 miles to Gaviota State Beach Park. But neither option is particularly appealing, especially at night in shark-infested waters. So we build our campfire, set up the sleeping bags, and break out the bocce ball set for a quick game.

Bocce ball, as Derek likes to say, is Italy's gift to the world. It has become an integral part of our many surf trips. We've bastardized the game significantly to suit various beach conditions we encounter along the coastline. Basically, there are eight heavy resin balls, half the size and weight of bowling balls, and a smaller yellow "P" ball. A player is elected to throw the "P" ball after which the players alternate throws of their heavy bocce balls toward the "P." The goal is to hit the "P" with your bocce ball, which is worth two points. If nobody hits the "P," then the closest ball is worth one point. Game is to eleven. Games can be played with teams or by individuals. The "Thursday Rule," made up haphazardly on a late Thursday afternoon in Mexico, states that if a team is ahead by seven points or more, the losing team can call "Thursday Rule," which then requires the winning team to hit exactly eleven points to win the game, or go back to zero if they go over.

Every beach in California and Mexico offers its own unique playing field: sand dunes, cliffs, rock outcrops, dirt roads, canyons, tide pools, and so forth. Bocce ball has been a great source of inexpensive entertainment while waiting out tidal changes on countless surf trips.

At midnight, the ambers of our campfire fade as the poker game shifts financial wealth back and forth. Noticing several large boats approaching with floodlights pointed toward us, we dim our lantern and stare back intently, trying to make sense of their actions. I'm scared that this will lead to our having to vacate the property. The floodlights eventually turn off and the boats leave.

One of Santa Barbara County's sheriff commanders is a regular squash partner of mine and informs me that the boats were most likely operated by the Drug Enforcement Agency. The beaches stretching from Government Point to Santa Barbara are notorious drop off points for drug smugglers and some of the more significant drug arrests have been made along these shores. We proved harmless, evidently, and they moved on.

I love sleeping on the beach close to pounding surf with a large moon overhead. I awake a number of times during the night to listen to the surf and gaze at the star clusters, hoping to see the elusive shooting star. The near-full moon is extremely bright when camping 30 miles from civilization. The large set waves sound like they're breaking within a few feet of my sleeping bag and the beach vibrates slightly each time the tons of water come down on the sand. The smell of the drying kelp and salt water nearby is pungent. It is a smell that I welcome and feel relaxed around, like the smell of fresh-brewed coffee.

Occasionally, I flash on the possibility of a freak wave coming in while I'm asleep and dragging me out to sea in my sleeping bag, but quickly put that thought away as I listen, feel, and smell the rhythmic movement of the ocean at my feet, eyes closed. It's an awesome sensation and I'm thankful for where I am in the world. These are memorable moments.

The next morning at 5:30 A.M., with a tinge of that evil poker tequila still running through my veins, I awake and look out at the ocean. The surf has increased to overhead and the shape is flawless. Doug is awake too, and we quietly slip into our frigid wetsuits and paddle our surfboards out into the surf. The sky is just beginning to turn from black to blood red. Doug and I ride epic waves, and the world is as perfect as one could ask. For about an hour, we ride some of the best waves I have ever ridden, and I'm glad it's with my brother. Definitely one of the most memorable days of surfing in my 28 years at the sport.

The rest of the crew pull themselves out of their warm bags and paddle out. Together, the six of us surf flawless waves until 10:30 A.M. under an awesome morning light show. As the tide finally subsides, we paddle the surfboards in, break camp, and continue our kayak journey toward Gaviota.

The stretch of coastline from Government Point to Gaviota is, in my opinion, one of the most beautiful places on earth. The warm, undeveloped, rolling grassy hills of the California coastline look the same today as they must have looked 200 years ago to Father Junipero Serra as he established the California missions between San Diego and Carmel. Occasional sightings of wild boar, coyote, and red fox as we paddle down the coastline remind me how protected this section of the coastline is. The fact that it stretches approximately 15 miles is amazing. In time, I know that the land will be subdivided and developed and its beauty will be made available to more people, but not in the same condition that it exists today.

We paddle past various clusters of Hollister Ranch surfers, the first civilization we've seen in two days, as we head toward Gaviota. The fact that we have surfboards strapped to the back of our kayaks has identified us as trespassers in their minds and instead of acknowledging our "hello's" or "good morning" greetings, we get the proverbial "stink eye" from them as we paddle by.

Hollister Ranch beaches are accessible only to owners and their guests or by boat. The beaches along this stretch of coastline provide some of the best surfing in California.

Poor attitudes, unfortunately, are common among many Hollister Ranch surfers. The reports of hostility toward "outsiders" are numerous, and these surfers have made it part of their job descriptions to make life as miserable as possible for anyone from outside their exclusive gates. There are many other surfing locations that I know of that have this hostility toward nonlocals. But unlike those places, Hollister Ranch is a vast stretch of beach accessible only to those nonowners willing to make an adventure to get there, either by boat, treacherous hike, or kayak. I suspect their hostility has helped preserve the beauty of the property, on one hand, but it has also created an equally impressive nightmare in lawsuits, in-fighting, and general bad karma.

Derek has supplied me with a number of various recollections of past trips we've done together for this journal. The first story I'll interject is about looking to purchase land at Hollister Ranch some years ago.

CUATRO CASAS COMPANY
by Derek Levy

Dave, Lee, Todd and I formed this investment group. We all love the Hollister Ranch area so once we actually went with a realtor to look at ranch properties that were for sale. We happened to choose the worst possible day to do this: hot, sunny, not a whiff of wind, and all the surf spots were firing 4–6 foot perfection. Anyway, this realtor was a Hollister Ranch landowner/surfer who ended up being a real dick. In additional to showing us various parcels of land for sale, he began interrogating our surfing etiquette and outlining the unique rules that he helped establish. He was telling us that as a landowner, we couldn't bring more than one friend when going surfing and other such nonsense. So we started to mess with him. At one point, we were in a canyon and the realtor said that this was once a prehistoric lake. So I commented, "Can you imagine? A caveman in the water behind the boat yelling "Hit it, Thog!!"

Everyone laughed except you know who. Later, while watching perfect San Augustine Reef, I noted, with tongue in cheek, that this would be a perfect spot, right on this bluff, for a Taco Bell. The guys all roared with laughter but, needless to say, the realtor couldn't get rid of us fast enough. I got the feeling he wasn't too stoked.

Another appropriate side story at this point is about our original surf taxi, the *Campari*. The *Campari*, a 17-foot inflatable boat, was our access to surfing Hollister and Bixby ranches back in the early 1980's. On one particular day, the surf is 2–4 feet and we are motoring our way home, tired after a full day of surfing. Near a surf break called Utah's, we see a nice wave forming and Derek, driving the boat, is encouraged to ride the wave in the boat. "TAKE THE WAVE, SISSIE BOY!!" With the motor humming full throttle, we're buzzing along nicely on the wave (which is well overhead given our sitting position in the boat), everyone's holding on tight with adrenaline pumping and hair flapping in the wind. Suddenly everything goes dead silent as we're flying across the critical section of this wave. I look next to me into Derek's eyes and they're full round in horror. He reminds me of a character in an old silent movie of the 1930's. The motor's gone!! It fell off the back of the boat. Hysterical laughter is laced with fear-induced adrenaline as I stare at Derek's comical face, frantic about our $1,000 motor sitting on the ocean floor, and dreading the oncoming break of the wave we're riding.

When the wave eventually breaks on us, we are somehow pushed to the bottom of the wave, then pushed to shore sideways. We take an inventory on the beach and determine that the only thing missing is the motor. Evidently, the pitch of the wave torqued both the floorboards and the motor mount sufficiently to launch the motor off the mounting bracket and out of Derek's hands.

We swim back out to the general area where we last had the motor, looking for oil on the surface, swimming to the bottom, but no sign of it. We laugh long and hard back on the beach at the pure absurdity of the event.

On shore, we stumble upon a guy sitting in his car overlooking the whole incident. He is visiting his family that owns land at Hollister Ranch and is sympathetic to our current plight . . . four miles or so from Gaviota without a motor. He gives us a ride through the security guard gates to our car, we drive in and haul everything out. Twenty-five dollars at the gate to come in and retrieve our boat is a cheap price to pay relative to paddling the boat to Gaviota. Another adventure at Hollister Ranch.

There are so many wild stories about people who boat to Hollister Ranch. The boats generally tend to be small inflatables or small Boston Whalers, as they make for the easiest transport and launch from Gaviota. However, they also tend to be the most likely to suffer when problems arise. Horror stories abound of boaters being blown into the shipping lanes of the Santa Barbara Channel when the not uncommon hurricane force offshore winds howl along this coastline. While simultaneously trying to restart the motor and feverishly holding onto a surfboard that wants desperately to be airborne, you attempt to grab hold of huge chunks of kelp bed as you drift helplessly out to sea. Respect for these winds is equally prevalent in our kayaks, as we paddle relatively close to shore along this section of coastline.

After several hours of nonstop, relentless paddling, we're at a place called Little Drakes, not far from where we lost our motor some three years ago. Still no sign of oil coming to the surface, unlike the USS *Arizona* in Honolulu. The surf at Little Drakes is excellent, but is a locals-only place. The only time a boater or kayaker might consider surfing Little Drakes is when nobody else is out. To our amazement, nobody else is out on this Sunday afternoon. The sets are a solid five feet and it's breaking fast on the shallow shelf. Derek and John paddle their surfboards out and ride some beautiful waves. But it's not long before some people walk up to us on the beach and ask us to leave. We're trespassing, they inform us, even though we're parked on the wet sand. There is some heated discussion about what constitutes the mean high tide line and rather than go into it, we decide to leave. Much like a child who is told he cannot do something that he feels is right, I'm angry and am motivated to find a way to do that which I'm told I can't do.

As I continue my paddle toward Gaviota, I'm thinking (because you do a lot of thinking when you're long distance paddling a kayak), about this mean high tide issue. A light bulb goes on over my head with a potential invention. What about a cot-like device that creates a platform in the wet sand on which one could sit and sleep on and yet still remain in the mean high tide area? It could have four legs about three feet high that rest on Frisbee-type plates so that it doesn't sink into the sand too far, and with lightweight tubing and canvas, could open up into an area for

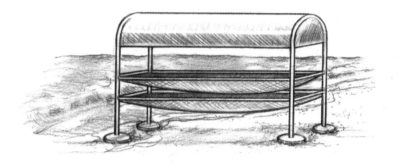

sitting and sleeping. A small shelf below the cot, but above the water could hold wetsuit, clothing and a surfboard. At high tide, the water might move gently below you, but you'd be high and dry on your canvas platform.

I further envision an entire beach full of these long legged cots on Hollister Ranch in the wet sand, some with sun umbrellas, and some with built-in tents. Perhaps even a high tide Taco Bell stand.

The paddle to Gaviota is a long one. I have no energy and am feeling nauseous, unsure if it's seasickness, food poisoning, the flu, or remnants of tequila. Throwing up between paddles, I've got to keep the kayak moving forward as we head toward the tiny dot on the horizon, the Gaviota Pier. Everyone else appears tired, too, after having surfed so hard in the morning. A warm, 15-mile-per-hour wind is at our backs and the wind swell is helping our progress, thank God. The sun is hot and we are battling a slight cross swell, which continually tosses the kayak in different directions. Six strokes on the right, one on the left, ride the oncoming wind swell for ten yards, then six strokes on the right, one of the left, ride the oncoming wind swell, over and over and over again. The arms are extremely tired; the paddle weighs about 80 pounds in my mind. A rudder would sure make riding these wind swells more productive.

One of the best things about paddling south toward Mexico, however, is that the ocean currents run north to south. Attempting to paddle north from Mexico to Point Conception would be ugly, I keep reminding myself.

At 4:00 in the afternoon, we finally reach Gaviota. We've just finished paddling 25 miles along some of California's most beautiful, undeveloped land. It feels great to be on dry land and stretch out the legs and back. Tired and hungry we take in some snacks before Lee and I drive his car back to Jalama Beach to get my van and trailer to haul everything home. Our journey is complete, a long haul but an excellent adventure.

A few months later, I contact the guys to see if they want to continue down the coast for a second leg, from Gaviota to Santa Barbara. Again, we will see some coastline that isn't readily accessible by anyone from Highway 101 and we might be able to surf some of the places rarely surfed. We agree to do a second leg in early November, 1995.

LEG TWO

GAVIOTA TO SANTA BARBARA
NOVEMBER 3–5, 1995

CREW: Dave Powdrell, John Beardsmore, Lee Walker, Derek Levy, Mark Levy, Michael Main, Jim Doughty

The crew for this leg is a bit different than the first leg, but no less interesting. Together, we hit Gaviota State Beach Park at 6:00 A.M. and meet the camp hostess, Ann, a retiree who saunters out of her trailer with baseball cap slightly askew. We do our standard "Eddie Haskell routine" with her and she plays a perfect June Cleaver. We're taking pictures with her and exchanging hats while haggling over an appropriate item to trade for her yellow government issue State Park jacket. Tough way to start a Thursday morning for her.

Our "Eddie Haskell routine" involves having harmless fun with new acquaintances on our various journeys together, which Derek and I have honed down over the years. We try to acquire something of value at little or no cost. Acquisitions to date include a coveted starfish button-down shirt acquired on a dance floor in Mexico, lifeguard shirts from a Del Mar Beach lifeguard, various U.S. Marine gear from soldiers, ties off various waiters, baseball caps, and earrings from pretty waitresses.

The "Eddie Haskell" also involves asking obvious questions to get a laugh while making new friends. For example, at the campground ranger station, a list of prohibited activities is usually posted on the check-in window.

> CAMPGROUND PROHIBITED ACTIVITIES!!!
> DOGS MUST BE ON LEASH AT ALL TIMES!!!
> CAMPGROUND LIGHTS OUT AT 10:00 P.M.!!!
> NO OPEN FIRES!!!

As we're filling out the forms and writing checks, we'll nonchalantly glance at the prohibited activities and begin the barrage of goofy questions, usually starting from the top.

Derek: Where's the best place to let our poodle run wild?

Ranger: Sorry, dogs must be kept on a leash at all times.

Dave: We'll be playing poker in front of our headlights at midnight tonight, can we deal you in?

Ranger: No. First of all, I don't play poker and second, all lights have to be out by 10:00 P.M.

Derek: Where should we keep our gasoline cans for tonight's bonfire?

Ranger: Oh you guys . . . . [rolling his or her eyes and forcing a short chuckle realizing what we're doing]

If there's a line of cars behind us and time is a factor, one quick question will typically accomplish the goal: "We're planning to cook our poodle over a bright, open bonfire at midnight tonight, where's the best place to store the gas cans?"

The art in Eddie Haskelling is knowing what's obnoxious and what's funny, who's receptive and who's not. Done tastefully, it can be comical. When on a roll with Derek, I've cried from laughing so hard and, most times, the rangers are laughing with us.

It's cold and foggy as we prepare to leave Gaviota Beach. The air temperature is about 58 degrees, the same as the water. The hillsides are covered in green grass similar to the Hollister Ranch

Jalama Beach, 6:30 A.M., 29-degree air temperature with 5-mph wind. A frigid start to the eventual 344-mile journey to Mexico.

Derek Levy with Point Conception in the background. We paddled next to three blue sharks along this remote, three-mile stretch of rugged coastline.

Doug Powdrell in front of the Point Conception Lighthouse, an unusual sight in an area known as Danger Area Nine in mid-winter.

Derek Levy on a classic Percos wave. We rode countless waves to ourselves from as far north as Point Conception to Tijuana Sloughs next to the Mexican border.

Derek, the consummate volunteer, hauled the bocce balls, horseshoes, food and other heavy gear that made paddling through thick kelp beds a struggle. Hollister Ranch in the background.

We encountered hundreds of California harbor seals, sea lions and elephant seals on the journey. During the Santa Barbara to Malibu stretch, great white sharks were reported to be plucking seals off the buoys. John Beardsmore checking for great whites.

Lee Walker provided us shelter from the onslaught of high tide at Emma K. Wood State Beach. Our campsite was nestled tight between the surf and the train tracks.

The shorebreak at Malibu beach was intimidating, but we all paddled safely through it. This turned out to be nothing compared to the eight-foot surf we'd face in San Diego during Hurricane Pauline later in the adventure.

Derek and the crew at Malibu Pier. Eighty-one miles to the Chart House in Newport Beach.

Paddling around Point Fermin in early morning thick fog, we came face to face with the huge freighter *Delware Trader*.

Tuna fish mixed with pepper sauce and Maui potato chips in a light mayonnaise dolloped on a French roll. Lunch on a remote Camp Pendleton beach.

Miles and miles of desolated beach at Camp Pendleton. We were fortunate not to run into any marines, who would most likely make us hike the kayaks up to the highway rather than allow us to launch back into the water. Richard Herald and the crew.

A typical poker night at Doheny State Park with cigars, tequila, and beer. Winnings typically include swim trunks, hats, sunglasses, pocketknives, sweatpants, and T-shirts. Men will be men.

With Mexico behind us, we salute our finish. Doug Powdrell, Derek Levy, Mark Levy, Tom Powdrell, Jim Doughty, Earle Powdrell, Lee Walker, Dave Baxter, John Beardsmore, Jason Huff, Richard Herald, and Dave Powdrell.

With the Tijuana bullring in the background, we complete the 344-mile journey from Point Conception. Approximately 344,000 paddle strokes and 51,600 calories burned over a 19-day period.

paddle of a year ago. Highway 101 is running with us now, however, robbing us of the privacy enjoyed on the earlier leg.

We paddle to an area known as the Garden Patch, an area with very clear visibility and a place frequented by skin and scuba divers. From the kayaks, we see dozens of colorful fish in three-foot deep water. Also a great lobster catching area, many divers describe watching lobsters mosey along the ocean floor here.

Continuing down the coastline, we pass a few relatively unknown surfing spots, Edward's and Seal's, that aren't breaking due to the lack of any swell. We paddle past numerous points and beaches that undoubtedly generate countless unridden waves, inaccessible due to the steep cliffs from the highway. The much-coveted waves of *The Endless Summer* are right under our noses, if we look hard enough.

Each of us paddles at our own speed and are spread out a bit as we inch our way down the coastline. In today's society, it seems that time is one of the most sought-after commodities. A kayak journey down the coastline provides me with the chance to think, to strategize, to contemplate, to reminisce, and to fantasize. This, I find, can be constructive to a point, but also mentally exhausting after several straight hours.

As the afternoon wears on, we eventually start looking for an evening camping spot. Finding a campsite is tricky as the important variables of dry sand, seclusion, easy access to and from the water, and firewood are not always easy to find, especially from a kayak outside the breakers. Additionally, as we continue heading south toward Los Angeles, the likelihood of finding these common variables continues to decline. Eventually we discover an excellent little shelf of dry sand along a sea wall 1/4 mile west of Refugio State Beach Park.

Watching everyone paddle their kayak to the beach reminds me of an awkward group of sea turtles getting rolled around in the waves trying to make it to the beach. It's also comical to watch the crew surfing their kayaks. Because they're so long and heavy, once these kayaks get angling in a swell, they tend to have a mind of their own. And no matter how hard you drag a paddle or lean to change directions, it's going its own way. So it becomes a matter of hanging on tight as the swell picks you up and breaks. It seems that, generally, one of two results occurs: the wave breaks, you stay upright in the kayak, and the whitewater pushes you to the beach. The other more common occurrence is that you're trimming along nicely, the wave breaks, and you flip upside down. There are paddles, hats, waterproof cameras, seat cushions, life jackets, sunflower seeds, and water bottles strewn along the beach, some being washed in to shore, some still floundering in the breakers.

Having scored three large live lobsters from my friend, Dan, at Ohana Fish Market in Goleta, we eat well with a steak and lobster feast that night. The beers are tepid, but the cigars are from Havana. We play poker with a $20 winner-take-all pot. Tequila shooters to anyone who misdeals or bluffs ineffectively; Michael Main quietly beats us all.

The journey continues the next morning toward Goleta. The seas are calm and our arms are sore. We do a little kayak surfing at Refugio Point with the few surfers there. The surf is a mere one foot, but it's fun. I attempt to get fancy with a takeoff to the left toward the rocks hoping to turn immediately back to the right and ride the wave. But, again, these kayaks don't understand the concept of turning when in the wave. I drag my paddle as hard as possible and lean with everything I have, but I am definitely going into the rocks. When the dust has settled, the damages are a broken paddle blade and a few cuts on the feet and legs. Which brings me to an important lesson . . . always bring along an extra paddle on these journeys. For the next two days I take three strokes on the left side for every one stroke on the right side due to the very minimal left paddle blade.

Paddling past El Capitan Beach, we eventually get to Naples, or Naples-by-the-Sea, as it was originally named back in 1887. Naples is an area next to Dos Pueblo Ranch, just west of Santa Barbara, with an interesting history. Briefly, it's an area of 872 acres acquired for $50,000 cash from the historic Den Estate by a wealthy high finance sort of fellow from Ohio, after wintering in Southern California. His plan was to subdivide the land into a tract of four blocks square forming a grid of over 250 numbered lots. His promotional brochures read:

> Pay no more exorbitant hotel rates! Own a cottage at Naples—take your family to the seashore in summer and rent it in the winter to Eastern families! The cottage will soon pay for itself!

The grand plan never paid off, though, and the property was never developed. Today, the property is close to getting final approval for subdivision into approximately five-acre parcels and it won't be long before Naples-by-the-Sea becomes the newest town on the Southern California coast.

We stop at Naples, eat a light peanut butter and jelly lunch, surf, and check out the land from the cliffs. There's a small tractor-made walkway from the beach to the land with appropriate No Trespassing signs. Naples is an excellent surfing beach not unlike parts of Hollister and Bixby Ranches. Although we surf in only 2–3 foot waves this day, Naples has the potential to hold large surf in the wintertime on a strong north swell.

I've asked all the guys to bring nine irons on this leg of the trip, as we'll be going past Sandpiper golf course. If we're lucky, we can sneak on to the infamous eleventh hole, consistently chosen as one of the most beautiful holes in golf, a par three dropping down toward the ocean. But the weather's great, it's Saturday morning, and the course is backed up with golfers. The clubs are destined to remain unused on this journey, sloshing around in the kayak hull. Rats.

Our journey continues in the afternoon past Isla Vista and the University of California at Santa Barbara. At Coal Oil Point, crude oil seeps up in large blobs through natural leaks in the ocean floor. It is the most disgusting $1/2$ mile of ocean we've encountered. The oil is thick, sticking to the sides of the kayaks, and stinks. There is also a large area about the size of a few football fields that is bubbling up natural gases. It's like paddling in a carbonated water field. The gases are odorless, fortunately, but it's a very strange sight paddling in this bubbling Fizzie field.

With the wind at our backs, we drift and paddle past the University of California, and Campus Point, beaching the kayaks at

More Mesa Beach. This has been the longest one-day paddle we've done to date, approximately 19 miles. We are all tired after paddling for close to six hours in addition to surfing at Naples.

More Mesa Beach turns out to be a nude gay beach. I guess we share a common objective with the nudists: finding a beach that's secluded, with dry sand, and where nobody will bother us. It's somewhat awkward for the seven of us, however, to change out of our wet gear into warm clothes with them watching us. As the sun begins to set, though, the nudists get dressed and leave. The vast, secluded beach is ours for the night.

Firing up the Coleman stove, we cook up simple spaghetti, eat surfer cookies (Flakie Flix), and swill warm Kern's fruit drinks. I suspect if my wife were with us, we'd have a beautiful goat cheese platter, roasted hot peppers with melted cheese inside, and be sipping a chilled Chardonnay. Men are generally satisfied with full stomachs and little work, and we are content tonight.

With the campfire blazing, we set up the poker table (an overturned surfboard), distribute evenly the poker chips and cigars. Harbor seals are barking like a neighbor's dog in the night, but it's refreshing because this is their domain. The gentle waves wash up on the beach and the air is unusually warm as we alternate the deal and selection of the game. Lowball, five card stud, blackjack, no peekie, low spade in the hole, the poker chips wander back and forth among the winners, eventually eliminating those of us that have suffered poor hands, poor judgment, or the ill effects of the tequila. This crowd is ruthless as any misdeal, misstatement, or for that matter, any deviation from flawless poker etiquette requires the victim to take a pull from the bottle. The problem with tequila and gambling, as the owners of any Las Vegas casino will tell you, is that the more alcohol consumed, the worse the judgment and the greater the likelihood of another misdeal. It's a constant spiral downward into poker oblivion, with little chance of taking home the coveted $20 pot.

Derek: Seven card no peekie . . . Spanky McFarland [$1.00 Monopoly bill with Spanky's face on the front] to see your first card. . . . [All antes are made.] COWBOY!! . . . Any bet? [while brushing his hand back and forth across the table like a Las Vegas blackjack

dealer asking for insurance] No bet! Trey . . . laaadddy . . .
TREEEYY!!! Bets? [Hand motion again]

Lee: I'll bet Wayne Newton [$10 Monopoly bill with Wayne's
face.]

John: I'll see your Newton . . . and raise you Eddie Haskell ($5).

Dave: Doesn't he need to draw another card?

EVERYBODY LOUDLY: DRINK!!! [while passing the tequila
bottle to Dave for asking a stupid question]

Derek: Dew eh, Trey, Cowboy, COWBOY!! Bets?

Dave: Ward Cleaver [$20]. . . .

The poker terminology as defined by fellow paddler Tim Ritter
is as follows: Ace=Bullet, King=Cowboy, Queen=Lady,
Jack=Johnny, Ten=Ten Spot, Nine=Niner, Eight=Crazy Eight,
Seven=Schven, Six=Sisqua, Five=Fever, Four=Quatro,
Three=Trey, Two=Dew eh, Joker=The Clown, and any wild card
is known as "Stinky Squirrel" in reference to what Marv Albert's
mistress called his toupee when it fell off his head during an affair
they were having.

And the conversation continues through the night until someone ends up with the stack of monopoly bills, which are then
redeemed for the real $20 bill strategically placed on the poker
table. Side bets are usually made on the last hand. Swim trunks,
pocketknives, and hats are last hand bets of the evening.

Composed, Michael Main quietly whips us all again in tonight's
game. I'm considering issuing him an IRS Form 1099 after the
trip for his gambling winnings.

The next morning the fog is dark, still and thick. Everything's
soaked as I stroll down the beach. Visibility is less than 50 yards,
a *Hound of the Baskervilles* scene. I've strolled out of sight of our
camp and the silence is loud. Even the surf is nonexistent. I imagine if out at sea in our kayaks with no landmarks in sight and
without a compass, one could quite easily paddle in circles or
straight out to sea. To quote John Dowd in *Sea Kayaking: A Manual
for Long Distance Touring*, "When fog has obscured land, one must
combine total knowledge of all forces affecting passage and hold

course accordingly. The inability to see can rapidly undermine confidence, if not prepared. One must listen intently for surf or boats while simultaneously watching swell direction."

I understand now why blind people have such incredible senses of touch, smell, taste, and hearing.

As the fog eventually lifts, we break camp and paddle two miles to Hendry's Beach in Santa Barbara for a Sunday brunch at the Brown Pelican Restaurant. Mark takes off in a flash knowing there's hot gourmet coffee and has the best table overlooking the beach for us when we arrive. A quick rinse off at the showers behind the restaurant, we settle in to Belgian waffles, eggs Benedict, fresh-squeezed orange juice, and unlimited hot coffee. This beats the heck out of the three-day-old, slightly saltwater-soaked Danish rolls sloshing around in the bottom of my kayak, the original breakfast planned for the day.

The hostess, Wendy, and our waitress, Amy, giggle as Derek has an art for flirtatious behavior that is unrivaled, in my opinion. He has both girls sitting on his lap while we take pictures and share stories. He's wearing his pouting face looking sheepishly into their eyes, like a lovesick teenager. With Derek on a roll, he becomes the morning entertainment for the patio seating and everyone gets a good laugh.

We're back at sea heading toward the Santa Barbara Harbor with full stomachs. Some of the palatial estates of Hope Ranch and Santa Barbara can only be seen from the water, and many are quite remarkable along this stretch of coastline. Clearly, the wealthy enjoy oceanfront property and I can only imagine where the tens of millions of dollars come from that allow the typically all-cash purchases of these homes.

I have made it a point to be on good terms with all persons, part of a creed from the Desiderata, a gift from my mother decades ago. The Desiderata is what I refer to as a one-page Bible, describing a code of ethics and morals that I try to subscribe to. But for some reason, Jim rubs me the wrong way, the same way Newman bugs Jerry Seinfeld in the television series. As we paddle down the coastline toward the Santa Barbara Harbor, he relentlessly spews Rush Limbaugh monolog to me with zero tolerance for any other point of view and a smirk of superiority on his face. He's like a brainwashed robot, and, I believe, enjoys antagonizing me knowing that I am the treasurer and accountant for our Democratic Congressman, Walter Capps, one of my clients, and, more importantly, a wonderful human being.

Jim is convinced that Democrat means liberal, which means freeloader, and that all Democrats are less American than Republicans are. I'm a lifelong registered Republican, but on the moderate side of the table. I'm a strong supporter of fiscal responsibility but a humanitarian when it comes to helping those less fortunate. Not wanting to listen to his hostile, abrasive remarks, I quickly paddle on ahead. He then paddles up behind me attempting to knock my kayak upside down, not a pleasant thought given the weight of the kayak, and the fact that I'm tired and cold. For the next three miles he continues to rear-end my kayak, ram my kayak at full speed from the side, and basically piss me off. I keep him at bay with my paddle and make it to the beach without being flipped over, which pisses him off.

On the beach, I try to make amends with him and extend my hand for some kind of reconciliation, but he won't shake my hand. Evidently, I learn from the other guys, my kayak had bumped his a day earlier, although I do not recall the incident at all, and he had fallen out of his kayak. He was simply getting even with me. I'm convinced his aggression was due to our political differences. I guess we tolerate each other now when we see each other at social events, but it's not a comfortable relationship for me. Maybe there's more to it than what I know, but he hasn't shared it with me. This is a bad way to end what was previously a great paddle for me. There are inevitably personality differences when groups of people get together. The art is listening, communicating, and tolerating, but sometimes it's harder than other times.

At Stearn's Wharf, we paddle into the harbor mouth and are met by our lovely wives. Total distance on this leg is approximately 40 miles. Total cumulative distance is 65 miles.

LEG THREE

SANTA BARBARA TO MALIBU
JUNE 14–16, 1996

CREW: David Powdrell, John Beardsmore, Lee Walker

This leg of the journey down the coastline is going to be a long one, approximately 76 miles in three days. The crew is thinned down to the hard-core group. Our prior best had been 19 miles in one day and that was fairly brutal. We'd now be doing three consecutive days at 25 miles plus. The crew is also thinned out as Derek, Mark, and fellow paddler Tim, have flown to England to attempt a world record English Channel crossing on paddleboards. Along with three other Manhattan Beach paddleboarders, they, in fact, set a new world record time by crossing the 23-mile channel in 6 hours, 29 minutes.

We hit the water in the Santa Barbara Harbor at 5:30 A.M. The sky is just turning light and it's going to be an excellent weather day. The media has been airing and printing a number of articles in the past two weeks about great white shark sightings between Santa Barbara and Ventura, our first day's paddle. Evidently, the seal population has been growing along the coastline and that has, in turn, lured the sharks. In fact, there have been dozens of seals that have boarded sailboats in the harbor. At least one boat sank from the weight of the seals.

I've taken my two children, Keenan and Madison, to the thrift store to select some "chum" for the great whites. We've picked out two stuffed animals; a dog and a bear, and a Barbie doll for 99 cents. We tie rope to each of the chum's ankles and to each of the three kayaks. "If the great white shark comes near you," I tell John and Lee, "you simply toss your chum out and pray."

On a recent Father's Day, I asked my daughter why she thinks I'm weird. "Because you're funny, Dad. You play with my dolls and bug me in the mornings." I am the consummate "Disneyland Dad," the term that describes the father who loves to play more than to discipline. When reading stories to my children at night, I get into character voices while frequently replacing the important character names with the names of my children and their friends. The princess's name becomes Madison, Keenan is the brave warrior, the beautiful queen is Valerie; Bartley, our dog, is the fire-breathing dragon, and I'm the crazy magician. And if a particular story isn't going in the direction that I think most appropriate, I like to improvise to a more interesting finish.

I suspect that the demise of my own parents at a young age is a significant factor in my outlook on life and behavior with my children.

My father died tragically in a fire when I was five years old. I do not remember much about him or the accident. Evidently, the blanket on his bed was up against a wall heater as he went to sleep that cold October night in a small hotel in Genoa, Nevada.

My three brothers and I, ages 2, 3, 5 and 6 at the time, were lovingly raised by our mother. She was an incredible lady who built a multimillion-dollar real estate development company on 200 acres of land in Carson City, Nevada, while simultaneously raising four young boys as a single parent. To this day, I do not know how she did it all. She, too, died tragically young from the effects of multiple sclerosis, a terribly cruel disease. She died penniless after years in hospitals and nursing care facilities, having inadequate health insurance at the time she contracted the disease at age 37.

Holding my mother's hand and talking with her throughout the afternoon of her death was one of the most painfully beautiful experiences in my life. Her final wish was for me to buy a case of champagne and distribute a bottle to each of the nurses employed at the nursing home; in celebration of the life she had, the new life she was about to enter, and as a thank you for all the wonderful care she was provided. I think I cried for two straight days after she passed away. Sitting at the Brown Pelican Restaurant at the beach in Santa Barbara after her death, a storm passed overhead and the entire sky will filled with small arching rainbows, a final good-bye kiss from her.

I can't tell you how many times I've asked the question, "Why would a loving God condemn young, beautiful, productive people to an early, sometimes cruel death?" I think, after all these years, I'm starting to figure it out, at least in my own mind. It's to remind us, like a cold slap on the face, that we survivors are blessed to be on this earth; that we must enjoy each and every day as if it were our last; to laugh whenever possible and to love yourself, your family and your friends. The current Nissan motorcar slogan sums up my overall outlook on life, "Life's a journey, enjoy the ride." This kayak trip is part of that philosophy.

Paddling hard for a solid four hours, we beach the kayaks at Indicators, at the backside of Rincon Beach. We've gone about 14 miles and I can already tell this is going to be the kayak trip from hell. After an early lunch on the beach, we head back out and continue the paddle past La Conchita, Mussel Shoals, Seacliff, Hobson's, Pitas Point, and finally to Ventura.

It's been eight hours of strenuous, continuous paddling with little conversation when we arrive at Emma K. Wood State Beach Park in Ventura. We locate a very small piece of dry sand next to the train tracks just north of the campground. Emma K. Wood State Beach Park is a campground for large group camping only, typically the Boy Scout and Girl Scout troops use the facility. Fortunately, no groups are using the grounds today and no park ranger is on site, so we are less likely to be discovered camping on the beach and forced to abandon it.

After hauling gear up the beach, I lay my head down on the ground tarp and literally pass out for close to an hour. I think I'm as physically exhausted as I have ever been in my life. When I awake, my muscles are sore and my butt is numb; thank God John has brought along his magic over-the-counter pain relievers, Orudis KT. We immediately rename them "Alrightas," or "Green Magic," after taking two, which dissolve the aches quickly.

Knowing that this leg is a long one, we elect to forego the heavier toys, including the bocce ball set. Hence, a more natural version of bocce ball is borne . . . surf bocce or rock bocce. The "P" ball becomes a small, easily identifiable seashell or rock and the throwing balls are larger individually identifiable shells, sticks, or stones. With a heavy "P" ball and lighter "throwing balls," surf bocce allows for "par two" and "par three" holes made at the election of the thrower. A par three hole involves throwing a heavy "P" way down the beach. Each player then gets three throws of one of their much lighter throwing balls. "Shotgun" throws can also be called at the whim of the "P" thrower whereby everyone throws all their "throwing balls" at the same time. Surfers are generally a simple yet imaginative lot.

We dine on pasta and lukewarm beer and knock out early for the night, foregoing any poker. Although we are tucked in tightly between the Amtrak train tracks and the pounding surf, we all sleep like babies throughout the night.

In the morning, we take a few more "Green Magic" before hitting the water. The paddle will be a long one again today, 25 miles past Ventura, Oxnard, Port Hueneme, around Point Mugu to the Big Sycamore State Park, below the Santa Monica Mountains.

Along the stretch between Ventura and Oxnard, I see seven dead seals either floating bloated on the surface of the water or lying on the beaches. It's hard to say what killed them, but they're more abundant here than anywhere else we've been.

Trash is also a common sight, not just along the Oxnard/Ventura coast, but along the entire paddle. Entire 33-gallon trash bags filled with trash are occasionally seen floating on the ocean surface. Plastic bags, foam, and plastic bottles wash past us and I can only imagine how much junk is on the ocean floor. For too many people, the ocean continues to be a sewer or a dumping ground, which is very sad to see. And I wonder how many of the seven dead seals I see today died from eating plastic, foam, or toxins, and how many from natural causes.

We beach the kayaks next to the military base just south of Oxnard for lunch. This is the military base that has the large sign on Highway 101: PACIFIC MISSILE RANGE—CAUTION, SHOOTING RANGE, LIVE FIRE. Fortunately nobody is taking target practice as we saunter through the open fence onto the military base for a short photo session.

After lunch, we paddle into the Channel Islands Harbor at Port Hueneme. This is a huge harbor with thousands of boats. After talking with a fellow kayaker at the harbor mouth, we head in for some coffee at the 24-Hour Tackle Shop. Amy, the cute young blonde, is on the telephone calling out yesterday's official fish catch to the newspapers: " . . . 26 rock fish, 124 mackerel . . . ." Suzanne from Reno looks more weathered, like she's had a drinking problem in the past and has smoked a few too many cigarettes. The two missing teeth in the front of her mouth don't help her appearance. But they're both sweet ladies and we share laughs with them over hot coffee. A quick game of pinball and we're back on the water.

We paddle the rest of the afternoon toward our destination, just past Point Mugu. The last mile feels like ten. We're exhausted and around every bend we hope to find dry sand, but the strong shorebreak continues to pound on the rocky shoreline. We make it around several points, hoping each is the last one. Finally, we find Big Sycamore Campground. The beach is packed with people enjoying the hot summer weekend afternoon and we crawl up looking quite shabby, I'm sure. We hike over to the park ranger who is unsure how to deal with us. "Sorry, the campground is full," we're told. He radios over to his supervisor to get some guidance on what to do with us. He informs us that the California park system has a relatively new arrangement for bicyclists and perhaps we can fit the criteria. For $5 per night, bicyclists can sleep at the campground regardless of availability and reservations.

The state park supervisor, a Courtney Cox look-alike, screeches to a stop in her new government-issue Suburban a few minutes later and John and I "Haskell" with her, uneasy about the options we have should she decide we can't spend the night at the park. We laugh, flirt about staying at her house with her, and she eventually agrees to let us camp anywhere on the beach for a fee of $3. We find an open day-use picnic table and set up camp.

A large family, in both stature and quantity, is parked next to us listening to loud music, playing soccer, and cooking dinner while using a ten-foot telephone pole as firewood on the bar-b-que grill. Five of the neighbor children come over to visit and together we feed the seagulls our saltwater-soaked bread and play soccer with them. After a great steak and beans dinner, Lee, John, and I settle into some cards. The music next door continues to play louder, their lights are bright, but we know that they'll soon be leaving. The entire beach will be ours shortly.

At about 10:00 P.M. I knock out and am followed by the rest of the guys while the music, laughter, and lights continue at our neighbor's campsite, which keeps Lee awake most of the night.

The next morning, I find our neighbors sprawled out on the ground next to us, with the telephone pole smoldering on the ground. My walk to the outhouse enlightens me to the fact that the entire half mile of beach is deserted except for the neighbors from hell sleeping within a few feet of us.

Leo Carrillo State Beach, a few miles south of Big Sycamore Campground, is an excellent surfing break. This morning, there are 15 guys in the water and the surf is 1'–2'. The water in the bay at Leo Carrillo is pure glass. The kayaks are gliding across the water, and it's almost mesmerizing. For about a half hour, we're skating across this sheet ice and it's absolutely beautiful. My arms feel unusually strong now, I'm totally relaxed and in an almost transcendental state. The kayaks are flying across the water.

We align ourselves to our next target, Point Dume, which is barely visible some 11 miles away. Rather than hug the coastline, we elect to paddle directly toward Point Dume, getting into the rougher open ocean about five miles offshore. About two hours into this trek toward Point Dume, with the sun baking down on us, I'm reminded of a scene from the movie *Out of Africa*. Meryl Streep and Robert Redford are out in the middle of a hot, dry desert in Africa when out on the horizon a small band of colorfully attired African men is seen running across the super heated, mirage-like desert floor going from what appears to be nowhere to nowhere. We are that African tribe to the fishermen bobbing in their boats far out at sea.

The mind does quite a bit of thinking on a journey like this. The body is working hard in the hot, glaring sun and there's not much conversation among us. I think and rethink about my family, work, and friends. It's exhausting. I feel like I'm at a doctor's lobby without the benefit of the magazine rack. The wait lasts for several hours.

Suddenly I hear what sounds like a bad argument. I turn and it's John singing Elvis Presley's "Hound Dog" at the top of his lungs. He has unpacked a Sony Waterman, plugged it into his ears and is belting out tune after tune. I am both green with envy and simultaneously impressed by his lack of singing talent. I try listening to him but it's not a pleasant thing he's doing to these songs. I've got to get a waterproof radio for the next leg!

After four hours of open ocean paddling, we finally reach Point Dume where we find a secluded beach. It feels good to stretch the legs, eat some sunflower seeds, and drink water. It's very hot on the beach and it feels good to relax a bit. This would be a great beach to spend the night on, as it's very difficult to get to by land. There are other people on this beach, but they had to make a real effort to get down the cliffs or make a long walk in from the south.

Paddling toward Malibu, this is definitely a different world now. We paddle past a massive health spa on the cliffs with all the workout machines outside overlooking the ocean. The huge palatial estates, as well as the tiny beach cottages of Malibu Colony, are immaculate and impressive. These are the homes of the movie stars.

Eventually, we turn a corner and see the Malibu Pier. We head toward Alice's Restaurant where we meet our wives and children for an awesome Father's Day dinner. The beer at the bar is ice cold, the Chicago Bulls are winning the NBA playoffs, and the food is great. More importantly, it is great to be with Valerie and the kids. I'm truly blessed by a great wife who encourages me to take these trips and by kids who are anxious to paddle with us someday. Total distance on this leg is approximately 76 miles. Total cumulative distance is 141.

LEG FOUR

MALIBU TO NEWPORT BEACH
OCTOBER 3–6, 1996

CREW: Tim Ritter, Derek Levy, Lee Walker, Dave Powdrell, John Beardsmore, Doug Powdrell, Mark Levy, Dave Baxter, and Jim Doughty, Charlie Didinger, Craig Welday, Jim Cowherd

The logistics are getting more difficult now. There are now 12 people on this leg, we have six paddleboarders that are limited to what they can carry, and most important, camping accommodations along the coastline are getting very scarce. I've arranged rooms at the Marina Del Rey Hotel where we'll bunk for the first night. The Radisson Hotel in Seal Beach is where we'll stay the third night as there are no camping areas or safe places to bivouac on the beach.

Also new this trip, our wives have arranged a hotel in Newport Beach for the weekend. They, too, are looking forward to a mini-vacation.

Tim has been instrumental in arranging quite a promotional extravaganza for this journey. He's lined up a cocktail party/happy hour event at the Malibu Inn Restaurant and Bar on Wednesday evening and another event in Seal Beach at Hennessey's Tavern. He also issues press releases to the *Los Angeles Times*, *Santa Barbara News-Press*, and *Seal Beach Sun*. And finally, he makes up

sweatshirts and T-shirts, compliments of Hennessey's Tavern and
Fat Face Fenner's Faloon in Hermosa Beach. Tim has a new nickname . . . Don King.

The boys begin arriving at the Malibu Inn Restaurant and Bar
at around 5:30 P.M. Doug has driven down from Sacramento with
his wife, Patty, and youngest daughter, Holly. John Beardsmore,
Dave Baxter, Jim Doughty, my wife, Valerie, and I have driven
down from Santa Barbara in two vehicles, a necessary evil in carrying kayaks and gear. Lee and Allison Walker, Derek, Mark, Tim,
and newcomers Charlie Didinger, Jim Cowherd, and Craig Welday
arrive from Manhattan Beach.

We swill beer and chomp tortilla chips listening to a burned-
out surf band crank out tunes at outrageously high decibels. There
are the sixteen of us, the band, and six Pepperdine University
students at the bar. It's great seeing the gang all together under
one roof and we're all anxious for the adventure ahead of us.

We haul the kayaks to the Malibu Pier and lock them to a
fence post behind Alice's Restaurant with my $2 cable bicycle
lock. After taking the important valuables out, I cross my fingers
that the kayaks won't be stolen during the night. The
paddleboarders elect to rent a room at a local hotel for the
paddleboards, as there is no way to lock them up with the kayaks,
and our hotel rooms are packed tight, six guys per room.

During dinner at the Malibu Inn Restaurant, we talk about the
upcoming trip. Kayak and paddleboard speeds are bantered about.
Jim's Valhalla kayak, a long, sleek, 20-foot rascal, looks exceedingly fast. He informs us that he has previously paddled 18 miles
in two hours, a speed that none of us would be able to match. The
Scupper Pros can manage between three and five miles per hour
and the paddleboarders claim a speed of up to five miles per hour.
It will be interesting to see how the various boat speeds differ
over long distances. We head over to the hotel rooms down the
street and get an early shuteye.

Thursday morning, 4:30 A.M. I can't sleep as those darn gears
in my head are turning, so I stroll over to Alice's Restaurant and
confirm that the kayaks haven't been hijacked while resting next

to Highway 1. The Jack in the Box drive-thru is open, so I order up 11 coffees to go. Felix is not prepared for such an order so we talk about life as a graveyard shift manager of Jack in the Box while he fires up the four coffeepots.

"I see all kinds," he informs me. "Pepperdine party animals with the munchies, night surfers, movie stars. You name it!!" I'm beginning to wonder if there might be a career opportunity for me at Jack in the Box, I tell Felix, as I casually glance down at the HELP WANTED sign below his left arm. After sharing with me the many benefits of working for Jack in the Box, the coffee is perked. "I'll think about it, Felix. Thanks." I head out with my three trays of coffee dripping scalding hot liquid down the front of my white T-shirt.

It's pitch black outside but I can see that the surf at Malibu is three to four feet as I stroll down Pacific Coast Highway. No cars on the highway, but there are 12 surfers in the water. I watch a few sets from Malibu Pier before continuing my stroll back to the hotel.

I reflect back on the night surfing sessions at Malibu Beach with my brothers years ago. We'd paddle out into the surf at midnight under a full moon. The phosphorescence streaming from the fingers with each stroke in the water is truly beautiful. Choosing a good wave at night, however, is intimidating with only an approaching dark horizontal line as a guide. When the swell is big, it is downright scary, as occasional set waves will break unexpectedly within a few feet. We'd typically paddle in to the beach by 4:00 A.M., saunter across the street to Jack in the Box for tacos, orange juice, and coffee before heading home.

I've always been a morning person. The mental gears start moving in my head at between four and five every morning and there's no way I can continue to sleep once they go in motion. At home, this usually means that I wash last night's pots and pans, empty the dishwasher, read the newspaper, eat my cereal breakfast and talk with Bartley, our dog, all before 5:30 A.M. I usually slide onto Madison's or Keenan's bed at around 6:00 A.M. and start reading a story out loud to wake them up, or I'll get out two or three of their favorite animal dolls and put on a skit on the bed. Valerie usually comes running in with "LET THE CHIL-DREN SLEEP, HONEY, IT'S SATURDAY MORNING!!!!" Even on weekdays, I have to let them sleep in to 7:00 A.M. before I can go in to wake them up. If I could, I'd wake them up at 5:00 A.M. every morning and we'd play Scrabble, spades, or read a story together.

Everyone arises in the hotel room at around 6:00 A.M. and we head down to the hotel lobby for their continental breakfast, which turns out to be an awesome spread of fresh fruit, juices, cereals, bagels, coffee, muffins, and complimentary newspapers. We look somewhat out of place in our wetsuits eating everything on the buffet table. Had the management known that we had six people in each room, I doubt we'd get carte blanche at the break-fast buffet.

We finally make it to the beach and prepare for the first day's paddle. A few pictures are taken while we try to cram everyone's gear into the kayaks. Turns out we have plenty of room given the fact that our food and camping supplies are minimal. Tim's cousin, Jason, has volunteered to truck the sleeping bags to Palos Verdes for us, which helps out tremendously.

The water temperature is about 63 degrees, and the sky is over-cast. The set waves pounding on the beach are intimidating, but we all make it safely past the breakers. The paddling begins to-ward Marina Del Rey, some 14 miles south. The paddleboarders start off quickly while the kayakers get water bottles, cameras, stereo headphones, and snacks arranged on board. I'm most con-cerned about Dave Baxter as it's his first attempt at long-distance kayaking, but when I look over at him, he's paddling like a pro. In fact, he's well ahead of many of the veterans. John Beardsmore takes the back position, which I appreciate, because I know he could paddle to Hawaii, if he had to.

With a crew of 11 in the water, there are plenty of varied dis-cussions available. Small groups of two or three guys work their way down the coastline in conversation. I really enjoy the fact that everyone has a unique perspective of the world and certain things that particularly interest them.

Mark Levy is constantly searching for more speed in his paddleboard. The pros and cons of small channels running down the bottom of the paddleboard are bantered around. A thicker nose and thinner tail section, wider vs. narrower, longer vs. shorter, body position on the board, and so on. As Derek describes him,

> Mark can't throw a football or a baseball worth crap and he can't play volleyball or shoot hoops any good either. But if Mark puts his mind to an individual sport, watch out. He won the U.S. Surfing Championships in 1974, has run multiple marathon races including the Boston Marathon, and swum the Hermosa to Manhattan Beach Pier race in 36 minutes (Derek trained his butt off and it took him 59 minutes).

> In the 1996 Catalina Island to Manhattan Beach paddleboard race, competitors from around the world were entered with the top 60 qualifiers allowed to compete. The conditions for paddling were terrible with whitecaps blowing on the water by 6:00 A.M. (The race was titled The Paddleboard Race from Hell in *Surfer's Journal* that month). Mark paddled 32 miles in this junk as hard as he could. Toward the end, he was in a race for first place with Kyle Daniels, a 20-year-old lifeguard from Torrance beach. Mark was paddling from the south along the surf line while Kyle was approaching straight from the west, the winning line on this particular day given the wind and wave conditions. Mark showed great sportsmanship congratulating Kyle and the fellow competitors and was equally stoked with his second place finish.

As we paddle our kayaks along, Derek and I inevitably talk about our families and the families of friends we have and how very lucky we both are. We both thrive on putting together various expeditions and family outings for our mutual friends and their families and we reinforce each other on the importance of staging these various events. We march in Santa Barbara's Summer Solstice Parade each year with the kids, Derek holds an annual Beach Decathlon, Valerie and I hold an annual Geriatric Surf Festival, and we do our occasional surf/camp expeditions. I suspect that when we're old and decrepit, we'll think back on these adventures and share lots of laughs. Our poor grandchildren will have to listen to these stories over and over and over again.

Derek and I connect in the humor category. For that matter, we all do. And when we get on a roll, I end up with stomach cramps and tears in my eyes from laughing so hard. It's the absolute best antidote to any ailment.

MEXICO WITH THE MOTORHOME
by Derek Levy

We made three or four full-on trips to Mexico in Lee's stepfather's motor home. Ugly Americans yelling "Somos rico, tu es pobre!!" We'd go searching for surf south of Ensenada as far south as El Rosario. On one of the trips, we pulled in somewhere for the night. A man comes out to meet us. He told us his dog's name was Duke. He said he was a lawyer and even showed us an I.D. He charged us $2 to sleep the night there. The next morning we wake up to realize that we were in the middle of the town dump.

One of our favorite surfing spots was a place called Uno Duno. This was a beach break with good southern exposure. The campsite was ideal for a few good reasons. The motorhome could be parked level on a dirt track just off a 70-foot cliff/river cutout. The view was awesome!!! The bocce terrain was great and also there was plenty of room for horseshoes. On a few of these trips, we took motorcycles and reconned the surrounding area or the road ahead. Once I remember Lee, Dave, Johnny Ludlow, and I with four surfboards, all on one motorcycle jamming down an endless low tide beach looking for surf. I also remember cruising the dirt tracks right off the beach. Once while riding double with Dave steering, we were scooting along pretty fast when the dirt track suddenly turned. Dave missed the turn and we flew (like Evel Knievel over Caesar's Fountain). We ended up flying over a gnarly patch of cactus about ten feet wide. Luckily we landed cleanly on the other side and kept going.

One night at Uno Duno we had exhausted all of our beer, tequila, and the motorhome's stock of liquor while playing cards. Drunk, we decided to play horseshoes, so Lee maneuvered the motorhome so that the spotlight could help us see. We ended up playing buck-naked on the side of the cliff. I even remember Lee (Brother Paco) got a ringer!!!

Another night Nico showed up. Nico was a local lobster fisherman who became friendly with us while we were playing cards. He liked our beer. He also took the longest pisses every five minutes that I have ever seen. Poor guy was complaining "Mi esposa." He was super drunk when he finally stumbled off. He was up early the next morning, however, because we saw him coming in from fishing at 7:00 A.M. (we were playing bocce). Nico gave us a friendly wave and went on his way.

After about three hours of paddling from Malibu Pier, we are at The Jonathan Club, an exclusive, private Los Angeles Beach Club, where Lee and his family are members. Lee cautiously volunteers to allow us to paddle in and sip a mint julep or two at the club before continuing on our journey. But the surf is a bit intimidating, it's rather cold, and it's only 10:30 A.M., so we all agree to continue down another two miles to the Santa Monica Pier to have lunch. Lee is relieved.

Lee comes from a very affluent family, Rolls Royces and memberships at exclusive country clubs. One of the things that I've always appreciated about Lee, though, is that he doesn't carry those airs of superiority about him. Although I know he appreciates the finer things in life, I suspect he may be more comfortable with the simpler things, a decent beach chair, a faithful surfboard, a well-worn sweatshirt, his beautiful wife near his side, and maybe a pair of old running shoes.

I've always treasured our friendship together through the years. He was with me when both my mother and stepfather passed away, important moments in my life. In years gone by, we've had a number of those heart-to-heart talks that only great friends can share.

The surf in front of the Santa Monica Pier is big, but not quite as scary as the beach breaks we've been paddling past for the last four hours. We safely paddle in for tuna fish sandwiches. We've developed a unique recipe for tuna fish sandwiches over the years.

Ingredients:

2 large cans of tuna in light spring water

1 jar light mayonnaise

1 bottle Santa Barbara Pepper Sauce

1 bag Maui thick-style potato chips

1 loaf bread

Tabasco sauce to suit taste

Drain water from tuna. Mix tuna, mayonnaise, and entire bottle of pepper sauce. Add Tabasco to taste. Stir to a flaky yet creamy texture. Dollop tuna mix onto bread. Take a handful of potato chips and place directly on top of tuna mix. Place top piece of bread on top. Press down firmly but evenly listening to the chips crack into the tuna mix. Bon appetit.

The key to a great tuna sandwich is in the pressing, in my opinion. This brings me to another of Derek's stories:

HYDRAULIC TUNA SANDWICHES
by Derek Levy

We were up in San Simeon on a beautiful hot weekend with Dave, Lee, and Pinky. One late morning we were surfing 2–3 foot Santa Ana condition waves at Bleshu Reef (right in front of the miniature golf course). Dave gets out early. The rest of us come up about 45 minutes later and Dave was busy making lunch (and had a plan). Dave had a big bowl of tuna fish mixed with hot sauce with a loaf of bread and a bag of potato chips (our standard recipe). He instructs Lee to listen to Pinky's and my instructions ("Stop!!" and "Go!!") in lowering the "feet" of the motorhome's hydraulic leveler. Dave proceeds to take a dollop of tuna on bread topped with a handful of potato chips then finished with a top piece of bread. That's a sandwich, right? But there's a twist. Dave then takes the sandwich and puts it between two sheets of waxed paper. Now Dave crawls under the motorhome and tells Pinky and I when to lower the hydraulic foot and when to stop. We relay these instructions to Lee. Some sandwiches get totally smashed until we get into a rhythm. Soon we're ending up with perfectly pressed tuna fish sandwiches. A few people gather to watch what we're up to. Dave bums a cigarette from a girl watching. An indelible image was burned into my memory . . . Dave halfway under the motorhome with a cigarette (long ash) hanging from his mouth and a squint in his eye yelling "Hold it, Hank!!" in his best auto mechanic worker voice while pressing tuna fish sandwiches under the hydraulic foot. Pretty hilarious.

Mark and Derek secretly head up to the Santa Monica Pier and come down with 11 bags of the best french fries I ever tasted. Unfortunately, the carnival rides on the Pacific Ocean

Pier are closed for the day, so we finish lunch and head back out to sea.

Timing is everything when paddling out in large surf. Doug and I head out together and work our way through the white water. A lull appears and we paddle hard to get outside. We both see a set looming on the horizon. Doug stops to wait out the set while I decide to scratch like hell to get over it. I watch helplessly, though, as the first set wave continues to build. Paddling with everything I've got, I know I made the wrong decision as the wave continues to build in front of my eyes. The wave breaks directly on my bow. I'm immediately flicked out of the kayak and go through the proverbial washing machine. Upon surfacing, I see my hat bobbing next to me and my kayak upside down gliding toward shore in the whitewater, some hundred yards away.

We continue on toward Marina Del Rey. It is on this next three-hour stretch of coastline that I learn to appreciate the beauty of the Speedo Water Radio, a waterproof radio the size of a half dollar that clips to your hat with two earplugs that slip into your ears. I'm sure there are purists who believe in the natural beauty in the sounds as you paddle, but there's also a strong argument for listening to KRTH 101.1 oldies at high volume while paddling.

While listening to the radio, I'm reminded of a study in a business management class I took while attending the University of Colorado. The study shows that when a new stimulus is introduced into a work force, the productivity of the work force increases. Music is the common stimuli in the studies. In fact, the inverse is also true. In a work force that has played music for years, when it ceases, productivity increases. I know that having the music in my ears on this paddle is good and I'm fairly confident that my productivity is increasing.

We turn into Marina Del Rey Harbor, which the hotel brochures claim is the largest marina in the world. It's another two miles in the marina until we eventually find Stacy of the Junior Lifeguard Program of Marina Del Rey. I met Stacy via telephone when organizing this leg of the trip. She greets us on the dock and is most gracious. The kayaks and paddleboards are stored in her enclosed freight container at the water's edge for the night.

We hike about a mile to the Marina Del Rey Hotel, which is inundated with Hollywood movie trucks and vans for the filming of *The Tracy Ullman Show* for HBO. After checking in, we catch a bit of the World Series before heading over to Aunt Tizzie's Back Porch for dinner. Aunt Tizzie's is owned by a black couple, which was recommended by our bartender, a beautiful black woman, Jeannie. The menu is comprised of grits, turnip greens, black-eyed peas, mashed potatoes, ribs, and chicken, and served in huge proportions. It's between 130 and 138 degrees in the restaurant, a special effect, I'm sure. So here we are, the only white guys in this packed restaurant, sweating, drinking Dixie beers, standing on our chairs singing "Happy Birthday" to a fellow patron, and having a great time with the patrons, manager, and waitresses.

After dinner, we head back up to our rooms only to find the film crew, actors, actresses, lighting crews, a fire marshal, and various other film crew in the room directly across from ours. This is a great opportunity for Derek, John, and myself to get a bit part in the movie, we're thinking. Unfortunately, this particular scene involves only two ladies in the makeshift office environment so we're out of luck. But we Haskell our way into the official jobs of calling out "QUIET ON THE SET!!!" and "ROLLING!!!", just before the cameras roll. We introduce ourselves to the director, the former Squiggy of *The Laverne and Shirley Show*. We also get to meet the woman who speaks the Marge Simpson voice on *The Simpsons*. The young lead actress in the film takes photographs with us but is generally a bitch. She's crying scene after scene, and the crew ends up shooting this scene over 12 times. We become fairly proficient at our jobs. "QUIET ON THE SET!!" "ROLLING!!" At midnight, when the scene is finally "in the can" and the crew is packed up and gone, Derek and I march directly down to the lobby to complain about all the noise of the film crew, particularly three fellows yelling "QUIET ON THE SET!!" and "ROLLING!!" at the top of their lungs in the hallway. With tongues in cheek, we demand an immediate reduction in our room rates. The hotel clerk knocks 25 percent off our two rooms, even though the second room was in another corridor of the hotel. We have some good laughs with her, as she is well aware of our antics.

Next morning, it's cold and overcast again as we unload the gear from the storage container. We've got a rather long haul ahead of us from Marina Del Rey to Abalone Cove at Palos Verdes. The two-mile paddle out the marina is beautiful . . . glassy water and impressive boats along the way. Out the channel and we're on our way toward Playa Del Rey, Manhattan Beach, Hermosa Beach, Redondo Beach, Torrance Beach, and finally Palos Verdes.

Lots of surfers are out at Hermosa and Manhattan Beach on this foggy morning. We get the proverbial "stink eye" from some of them but an occasional surfer asks questions. One fellow paddles his longboard up to me and shouts "Let's go!!" A bit leery, I'm wondering, does he want to fight me? "What do you mean?" I call back. "Let's race!!" he yells back. So I dig in and outpace him without too much effort. Stopping, I allow him to catch up, and I discuss our itinerary, past legs of the trip, and so forth. Like an excited child, he wants to come along with us right then. I encourage him to find some buddies and do something similar and he assures me he's going to do it. That makes me feel good.

Under the Manhattan Beach pier we catch a glimpse of Palos Verdes, or Rocky Point as it's listed on the marine maps. We head out a bit into the open ocean in direct line to our next destination, and I see two flying fish. The second one flies for a good 20 yards just in front of me. Tim sees it and comments about their relative frequency these days in these waters. I haven't seen a flying fish since traveling to the Caribbean decades ago. It's nice to know they're in these waters. I wish my children could have seen these flying fish with me, as they're such a unique phenomenon to me.

We paddle in at Bluff Cove, nicknamed Little Waikiki back in the 1950's. It's known for it's gentle surf but we've surfed it 6–8 foot back in the high school years. This was my favorite place to surf in the early 1970's.

Today, there are two guys in the water and they give us the full bad vibes. Derek catches a wave on his paddleboard quite a distance from them, and they both make some kind of disparaging comment about him. Again, this behavior is hard for me to understand. I put myself in their shoes and I try to understand their anger. I suspect a flotilla of 11 paddleboards and kayaks coming into what was once their quiet setting could be a bit frustrating. But it could also be a chance to learn something. The attitudes of California surfers continue to baffle me. Their poor attitudes are not going to preclude me from exploring and adventuring. Too many people are missing a bigger picture by closing their worlds to just their territories, thoughts, and beliefs. This is true in politics, religion, sports, education, and life in general, in my opinion.

Both Derek and Mark have had bad experiences with the locals in the past at Lunada Bay. Typically, one or more of the younger surf grommets flatten your car tires, break off your car antennae, rub surfboard wax over the front windshield, and/or break off the side mirrors.

Surfers are generally quite territorial, which can inhibit exploration. The study of surfer behavior would make for an interesting sociology paper. But more important, now's a good time for peanut butter and jelly sandwiches.

After lunch, we paddle back out and catch a few waves at the Cove. Mark rides a nice wave standing up on his paddleboard and Doug, John, Jim, Lee, and I catch a handful of head-high waves each before continuing the paddle south toward Abalone Cove.

The lobster traps are out in full force as lobster season officially opened last week. I count no less than 50 traps just outside Lunada Bay. Derek, Doug, and Mark catch a few waves at Lunada Bay. Because the surf is only five feet high, the break is treacherously close to the rocks at the point. Lunada Bay is an epic surf location at twelve foot plus. But today, a mistake on either a kayak or a paddleboard is sure to damage or completely break the vessel. The rocky bottom is lined with sea urchins, which leave sharp barbs in your feet if you end up walking to retrieve a lost board. But the guys all catch some nice waves without incident.

Doug has ridden Lunada Bay since 1969, when our family moved to Palos Verdes from Carson City, Nevada, but he does not condone the local behavior at Lunada Bay.

I have rolls and rolls of pictures of 20-foot Lunada Bay surf back in the 1970's when Doug was riding it with his pals, Frank and Angelo Ferrero, Bill Cagney, Joe Bark, Brian Nash, Kevin Barrett, Jeff Summerall, and Zen Del Rio to name a few. Dale Struble, a surf legend in our eyes, sold us fiberglass and resin to make our surfboards. It was a magical time.

We arrive at Abalone Cove, a few miles south of Palos Verdes, in the early afternoon and are met by Tim's cousin, Jason. He's got his pickup truck fully loaded with steaks, chicken, charcoal, ice-cold beer, and sleeping bags. After a hot shower at the lifeguard house, we set up camp, dine, and enjoy a brief period of sunshine, something that we haven't seen in two days. Everyone is tired, as this has been a relatively long stretch of paddling . . . some 21 miles.

After dinner we settle in on our standard poker game; a $20 pot, winner takes all. After two hours of play, it comes down to Derek and Dave. Derek throws down the gauntlet by raising the stakes. Final hand, winner takes all. If Dave wins, he gets Derek's hot sauce surf trunks. Dave throws in his Panama hat and his son's pocketknife. The winner also gets the $20 cash pot. Dave wins the game with three natural sixes. His nickname changes to "Damian," from the movie *The Omen* with the 666 inscribed in his head. To this day he wears his hot sauce shorts with great pride.

Craig Welday, a paddleboarder, joins us Saturday morning for the final two days of this leg. He arrives with ten cups of hot Starbuck's coffee and is an instant hero, at least with me. The fog is very thick as we begin paddling toward Los Angeles Harbor, Long Beach Harbor, and Seal Beach; visibility less than 100 yards.

After rounding Point Vicente and Point Fermin, we approach the entrance to the Los Angeles Harbor known as Angel's Gate. Our timing is impeccable as there are two tugboats coming directly at us with a major freighter, *Delaware Trader*, in tow. The tugs let the freighter go just in front of us and we are all quite close to this monster ship. Derek paddles to within ten yards of the ship and the contrast in boat sizes is awesome. The *Delaware*

Trader is approximately 2.5 million cubic feet of mass; our kayaks are about 30 cubic feet. I paddle near Derek and we call up to the deck hands and share greetings with the crew. Being next to this ship is like being next to a moving high-rise building. The sheer mass is striking. Fortunately, the ship has not accelerated enough to kick up a wake yet, so we have little trouble paddling in behind it and across Angel's Gate. Derek has to weave his way between the two tugboats and the freighter, however, as the tugs circle around to head back to the harbor. It's like watching an ant cross the freeway . . . but he makes it intact.

The next nine miles inside the harbor are the most tedious. We hug the rightmost part of the harbor next to the breakwall and paddle for what seems like forever. It's very foggy so the scenery is limited. The rock wall looks the same for the full nine miles. We eat lunch from the kayaks, as there's no place to land. The only things of interest along the rock wall are the starfish, crabs, and pelicans that watch us slowly navigate past them as the gentle swells rise and subside. I'm sure the pelicans are a bit curious at the situation passing by them, but like a good poker player, they keep their expressions to themselves. After three hours of uneventful paddling, we finally reach the exit of the harbor and can see Seal Beach some two miles away. It's a race to the beach for many of the paddlers while the rest of us trudge through the final stretch.

As we approach the Seal Beach Pier, the lifeguard speakers come alive: "ALL KAYAKERS AND PADDLEBOARDERS MUST PADDLE IN PAST LIFEGUARD TOWER 2." This is away from the swimmers and surfers but also further from the lifeguard house where we've arranged to park the kayaks for the night. The thought of having to carry these 250-pound. kayaks another half mile to the lifeguard house is a nightmare. But we adhere to their orders and survive the four-foot surf to the beach. Upon arrival at the beach, however, two lifeguard trucks and a very warm greeting meet us. The lifeguards load our kayaks onto their trucks and haul them to the lifeguard house for us. Again, a few telephone calls before the trip pays off handsomely for us. Steve Cushman, the captain of the Seal Beach lifeguard station, has taken good care of us.

We check in at the Radisson Inn Hotel before walking down to Hennessey's Tavern for complimentary drinks and dinner, courtesy Tim's connections. We power down just under $400 worth of free food and drink but 7:30 P.M. feels like midnight when you're extremely tired. We slink out of the bar with our tails between our legs as the band is setting up and the Saturday night crowd begins to arrive. Sissies.

Sunday morning, the shore break on the set waves is gnarly . . . four to five feet with eight-foot faces. While on the beach preparing to battle the shore break, a family of three saunters down next to us. They've got masks, snorkels, and fins on and waddle down to the water's edge. It's a comical sight because there is zero visibility in this treacherous surf and this family is very much out of shape physically. While Derek is getting ready to paddle out through the shore break, the wife wanders down the wet sand toward the water. She bends down to clear some sand out of her swim fin while a set wave looms on the horizon. Unbeknownst to her, the set wave jacks up, a full eight-foot face on this grinder, and slams directly down on her back. She's thrown around the whitewater, all diving gear ripped from her body, and she eventually washes up to her husband's feet like a large piece of driftwood. Then the line of the day comes down from a surfer (who has an uncanny similarity to Jeff Speccoli of *Fast Times at Ridgemont High*) on the pier who has witnessed this entire scene. "SEE ANYTHING GOOD?!?" he hollers down. His buddies roar with laughter. Before we leave Seal Beach, we glance back and see the divers sluggishly waddling back up the beach toward their parked car. It seemed like such a good idea at the breakfast table.

We're on our way toward Sunset Beach, Huntington Beach, and Newport Beach. The surf is building along the way. The surf report is calling it four to six feet on the sets. It would be no fun to either paddle in or paddle out through this surf, and fortunately, we shouldn't have to. At Huntington Beach, the World Championship of Surfing is in its third day of competition. As we paddle under the Huntington Pier, the announcer of the event comes on the loud speaker and broadcasts the fact that a group of kayakers and paddleboarders is on the way from Santa Barbara to Mexico. The crowd applauds our stupidity. In his broadcast, the announcer mentions Derek's and Mark's names, both familiar names in the competitive surfing world. We are all quite surprised at our brief notoriety and to this day, do not know how all this information got to the announcer's booth.

We make the final paddle to the Newport Beach Pier and take the customary finish line photographs in the water. Derek, Mark, Tim, and Craig paddle to the beach and hike to the Chart House Restaurant where we're scheduled to meet our wives in about three hours. The kayakers decide to continue down the coast to the Newport Beach Harbor and paddle directly up to the restaurant. What appears on the map to be about four miles from the pier to the Chart House turns out to be at least six miles, three of which are directly into the afternoon winds. Derek and Mark bodysurf eight-foot surf at The Wedge while we paddle the final stretch. We're all beat by the time we get to the Chart House, some 81 miles from Alice's Restaurant in Malibu.

We talk our way into scalding hot showers under the Chart House Restaurant using their garden hoses hooked up to the hot water heater before the families arrive. Fifteen of us have a great dinner, share war stories, and exchange awards. The paddlers each receive an award for their specific accomplishments during the trip. Derek, Tim, and I distribute the following awards, which are supported by refrigerator magnets with photographs depicting the various award namesakes. The awards are:

Wayne Newton Award: For the person who played the best poker on the trip or the person most likely to survive living in Las Vegas for a period of one year if abandoned there with only the clothes on his back: Dave "Damian" Baxter wins this award for pulling his three sixes to win Derek's shorts.

Rob Schneider Award for Man Behaving Badly: For the most disgusting person on the trip . . . .using old underwear as a coffee filter, that kind of thing . . . Tim Ritter, mostly due to his loud sleeping habits, belching, and other bodily noises.

Spanky McFarland Award: Initially designed as an award for the biggest eater on the trip, Doug received this award because he caught six beautiful sea bass from his kayak using only a string and lure tied to the side of his kayak while trolling various stages of the 81 miles. The fish tasted great at Abalone Cove.

Eddie Haskell Award: For the ability to schmooze complete strangers into thinking he's an angel and/or for the ability to obtain something of great value at no cost from a perfect stranger . . . Derek Levy, hands down. Derek can charm the socks off of anyone, but in a harmless, comical manner.

Ward Cleaver Award: For the most responsible guy on the trip. The person most likely to be called Dad, Commander, or Mr. Cleaver . . . Lee Walker. Lee is always the guy checking the weather conditions, tide charts, wind direction, making sure the coals are out at the fireplace, picking up the trash, and, most importantly, calling home and/or the office every two hours religiously.

Duke Kahanamoku Award: Clearly, the strongest overall paddler on the trip was Mark Levy. He works with the ocean rather than against it. Where he glides on the ocean, we push through it. It is always a thrill to be around someone that has mastered a task and converted it to an art form. Mark has done this on the ocean.

Hideo Nomo Award: Rookie of the year for 1996. Best new paddler and most likely to develop into an all-star paddler in the future. Tim Ritter wins this for his impressive showing on his first long-distance paddle over a period of several days. A close second place is awarded to Dave Baxter.

Miss America Award: Best evening attire, best swimsuit, and best personality . . . Jim Doughty. Jim was always able to look like the cover model for *Outdoor Life* each evening after cleaning up. His clothes matched, his hair was perfect, and he always looked refreshed.

Jim Kerrey Award: Best use of humor to combat fatigue and sore muscles on the trip . . . John Beardsmore for the line "No stamina, eh?", said to Derek Levy who casually mentioned that he was fatigued after the third day of paddling. John is a man a few words, but when he speaks, everyone listens. Someone gave him the nickname Lone Wolf on the trip, which also seems quite fitting.

Captain Joseph Hazelwood Award: Best crash or wipeout on a kayak, which may or may not have caused personal injury. I get this award for paddling through the set wave at the Santa Monica Pier and getting pummeled in the impact zone.

Mickey "Da Cat" Dora Award: For the most unusual, eccentric, and interesting guy on the trip; best storyteller around the campfire . . . Doug Powdrell. From his world travels and various college degrees, Doug has an incredible database in his head. Everything from celestial navigation to physics, he's always interesting around the campfire.

Don King Award: Best promoter of a sporting event while simultaneously maintaining an unusual hair style . . . Tim Ritter, for lining up all the evening events, team T-shirts, sweatshirts, and sponsors.

Total distance of this leg was 81 miles for the kayakers and 75 miles for the paddleboarders. Total cumulative miles on the trip to Mexico are 222. Approximately 123 miles to go before getting to Mexico. We've agreed that we'll break up the final miles into two legs, one in May 1997, and the final leg in October 1997.

LEG FIVE

NEWPORT BEACH TO DEL MAR
MAY 16–18, 1997

CREW: Dave Powdrell, John Beardsmore, Lee Walker, Derek Levy, Mark Levy, Richard Herald, Tim Ritter, and Jim Cowherd

I'm up at 3:15 A.M. to finish loading gear, having gone to bed at 1:30 A.M. By 4:00 A.M. John, Richard, and I are driving south toward Los Angeles. It's going to be a long day. We pick up Lee in Manhattan Beach and caravan with Randy, Tim, and Jim to Newport Harbor. After taking a few wrong turns near Newport Harbor, a lady pulls up next to us and asks if we're lost. The license plate on her Lexus reads KRZY KATY and she's either crazy or very confident to pull up to eight complete male strangers and ask if we need directions. We follow her through steep winding roads of exclusive Newport Beach neighborhoods and end up on the beach at the harbor. There's a chance we'd still be driving aimlessly in those streets today had she not volunteered her services to us. She's my first hero on this leg of the journey.

We're in the water at 9:00 A.M., a relatively late start given the 23-mile distance to be paddled today. The sky is cold gray and the waters outside the harbor are not smooth. Not a good sign this early in the morning.

Rookie paddler, Richard Herald, looks strong in his kayak and quickly begins to learn the nuances of kayak touring; how to hold the paddle, seating position, maximizing the paddle stroke, etc. As with Dave Baxter, I'm always concerned at first for the novices but, just like Dave, Richard does an awesome job keeping up with the veterans.

Long-distance kayaking is not fun like a day surfing or skiing is. In fact, as I reflect on it, it's mostly hard work. The heart rate is elevated for an extended period of time, as much as eight straight hours. It's more in line with a marathon run, or perhaps a long mountain climb. The exhilaration comes at the end of the day when you rinse off the salt water and put on cozy warm sweats, knowing you've just burned 5,600 calories and observed a unique perspective of the California coastline.

An hour outside of Newport Harbor, we arrive at Irvine Cove and Emerald Bay, two phenomenal private beach enclaves, with hand-raked beaches, and water toys galore ready for use by its wealthy inhabitants. The hillside above Emerald Bay was recently rebuilt after a major fire a few years ago. We "guestimate" the average asking prices of homes in these communities to be over $5 million. Discussion turns to the fact that throughout time, there will always be demand for beachfront homes but that these homes suffer the additional demands that nature puts on them: the continual expense to maintain the battle against salt water, winter storms at high tide for those homes sitting low near the water, the continual deterioration of cliff walls, and mud slides, to name a few. But given a healthy budget, living on the beach would be a wonderful luxury.

The entire distance from Newport Beach, past Laguna Beach to Dana Point is nothing but big, beautiful, expensive homes. It must be one of the most affluent portions of the California coastline.

We work past Dana Point, the former surfing mecca turned boat harbor, and paddle in at Doheny Beach, where Randy, Tim, Jim, and Jason meet us with ice-cold beer and bar-b-qued burgers. We play poker, smoke cigars, and do some of the other silly traditional things that grown men do when they get together. At 1:30

A.M. I hit the sack and am asleep within 20 seconds of putting my head on the pillow. It has been the long day that I had anticipated, some 22 hours earlier.

At 6:30 A.M., we're up. Lightning has been cracking throughout the night and it's a relatively gloomy day again. After cereal and orange juice, the four kayakers hit the water toward San Onofre, where we'll meet up with Derek and Mark. Tim, Randy, Jason, and Jim see us off before they head home in their cars and the Body Glove trailer.

Within a few minutes of getting on the water, a rainsquall hits, which refreshes me. The water all around us is bubbling as the raindrops hit the surface. The fresh water running down my face tastes good as I'm listening to a local radio station blare out some classic rock and roll. The "Alrightas" have kicked in and the muscles are feeling strong. This paddle will be a long one . . . 26 miles, which is our longest one-day paddle ever. The length of the paddle is many times dictated by the coastline and access to camping locations. With Camp Pendleton Marine Base along this stretch of coastline, a long paddle is required. Richard is a bit concerned as his wrist and hands are very sore. In fact, he has little or no feeling in some of his fingers. But he forges on without complaint. A real trooper.

Lee and John paddle hard and fast and get into "the zone." I suspect they're doing five miles per hour plus and are out of sight relatively soon.

The odd-looking San Onofre Nuclear Generating Station is coming within sight. Power plants require huge amounts of water to cool the circulating steam and sewage treatment facilities use the ocean for the disposal of treated effluent. We pass by several such facilities along the coastline. Given its bulbous shape, the San Onofre plant is the most unusual we've encountered on this trip.

A major surfing competition is in mid-stride when we paddle up to San Onofre. David Nuuhiwa, Herbie Fletcher, and a number of other impressive surfers from yesteryear are tearing up the 4–5 foot surf on longboards. We're quite a distance out from the surfers, but I hear some commotion on the loudspeaker on the beach and look out to see a set wave approaching Richard and myself. We both stroke perpendicular up the wave and barely make it over as it's cresting. It would have been very embarrassing to have been swamped by the wave and have to swim in for our kayaks, with hats, seat cushions, water bottles, and other various gear strewn out along the contest confines.

Camp Pendleton Marine Base encompasses the next 14 miles of coastline. Much like Hollister Ranch, it's like turning the clock back 200 years as we paddle along this raw, rugged, beautiful coastline. Fortunately, no military maneuvers are being conducted today, so we won't be dodging bullets as we move south.

If this military base was ever closed and the property sold to developers, there would be a significant supply of phenomenal ocean view property available. I suspect that the contamination and waste removal on the base could be an expensive proposition, however, given the many bombings and other military maneuvers that have taken place over the years.

At Las Pulgas, a campground located on the marine base with restricted public access by lottery only, we pull in for tuna fish sandwiches. The vast beach is desolate except for an occasional retired marine couple strolling along the beach heading back to their RV. We meet John and Cindy and their dog, Brownie. John's a retired marine sergeant who looks more like the lead guitarist for ZZ Top; overweight with a white beard down to his belly button. It's interesting how people sometimes move from one end of a spectrum to the other over time, having once been a young, fit, crewcut recruit.

John points out during our chat, "If the young marine guard drives down, you'll most likely not be able to launch back into the water. In fact, you'll probably have to haul the kayaks and paddleboards $1/2$ mile up to the highway and catch a ride to Oceanside. The marine guard," he continues, "is typically 18 years old and on a power trip. With his revolver in hand, he imagines he's on a special mission making sure that all enemy dogs stay on dog leashes, that no enemy surfer escapes into the surf, and that everyone on the beach must have a worse day than he's having."

And rather than risk having to deal with this young rascal, we finish our lunch quickly and head back out to sea.

Another one of Derek's stories, entitled "Sergeant Wilbur," is fitting about now.

SERGEANT WILBUR
by Derek Levy

At the south end of Camp Pendleton there is a camping beach resort for the marines and their families called Del Mar Beach. Randy Meistrell has a connection and got us on there for two nights. The place has a good south swell exposure and about ten of us got good 2–4 foot waves for the weekend. We became friendly with a few marines and their wives and ended up having a large bar-b-que with them on one of the nights. Later on that night, while we were around the campfire, a drunk marine named Sergeant Wilbur and a marine friend of his (who throughout the night did not say one word) stumbled up to our campsite. Sergeant Wilbur was a tank of a man, probably 5' 10", 240 pounds and solid as a rock. As the night progressed, Sergeant Wilbur taught us all how to salute properly and we sang great marine cadence songs under his guidance. He named Dave "Devil Dog" and Chris Evans "Hard Charger." It was pretty late and Sergeant Wilbur was starting to rage. Evidently, he was making quite a bit of noise with his bull of a voice and was disturbing a retired colonel who was in his motorhome across the way. When the colonel told Sergeant Wilbur who he was, Sergeant Wilbur immediately snapped to attention. The colonel was pissed and tore into Sergeant Wilbur about disrespect, the image of the marines, etc. As soon as the colonel was gone, Sergeant Wilbur split. Months later, Dave found out (Dave did some gratis tax work for one of the marines we bar-b-qued with) that Sergeant Wilbur had lost his stripes because of the campfire incident.

The afternoon winds are blowing fairly strong now, straight onshore. The ocean is lined with whitecaps as we paddle out through the surf. The winds are blowing at 15–20 knots, but it's a warm wind. The eight remaining miles to Oceanside Harbor are slow and arduous. Mark and I are paddling at similar speeds, but he's 100 yards further out than I am. From time to time, I turn to check on my progress with Mark and notice that he's frequently gone from sight behind the many large ocean swells between us. Then suddenly he bounces back up to the ocean horizon, arms working hard like mechanical windmills, with waves splashing over his back. These are definitely the roughest conditions we've faced to date and progress along the coastline feels exceedingly slow.

I suspect that most surfers and sailors have at least one hair-raising, near-death episode under their belt. Mine took place at Razorblades on the Hollister Ranch in December 1994. Derek and I and two friends, Paul and Jim, were huddled on the cold, windy, dark Gaviota Pier at 6:00 A.M. awaiting the opening of the mechanical boat hoist. Major storm warnings were being broadcast on the weather radio the night before, and we were hoping to catch the early part of the swell before the winds and rain hit. The swell size was 15 feet at the Point Conception Buoy and growing. We had the boat in the water by 6:30 A.M. just as the morning light was beginning to show. Gaviota, typically a calm water launch, was extremely turbulent and launching the boat was like riding a bull coming out of the shoot.

Working our way west, we had the swell and wind at our backs, an unusual phenomenon along this coastline. These conditions allowed us to make good time getting to Little Drakes. Completely out of hand, huge, gnarly storm surf was breaking at Little Drakes. It was unrideable. Moving on past Rights and Lefts, Utah's, and San Augustine's, we pulled up to Percos. Again, the surf was huge, dark, and angry. We decided it best to call it a day and head home.

Heading east we were now going directly into the swells and wind. The boat was constantly sent airborne before slamming hard on the trough of the oncoming wave. This relentless pounding continued for an hour while we continually took on water. Eventually, we were totally submerged sitting chest deep in water in our little Boston Whaler. Foam lined, Boston Whalers don't sink to the ocean floor, but our predicament was rather precarious. The crew went overboard while we all worked frantically to bail the water out. Somehow, we got the boat back on the surface, re-started the motor, and continued the slamming action east.

The boat submerged one more time and we repeated the procedures of exiting the boat and bailing water before firing up the motor and continuing toward Gaviota Pier.

With the Gaviota pier in sight, we were within $1/4$ mile of home when the motor died, not wanting to restart for anything. I immediately threw out the anchor and 60 feet of line, sufficient line to protect against drifting in normal conditions. But in strong storm conditions, you need a nine-to-one ratio of line to water depth. Ours was only three-to-one as we began drifting toward the rocks at Razorblades. We sent Paul and Jim in to shore on their surfboards hoping that they could catch a ride to the Gaviota ranger and get the boat towed to the Gaviota Pier. Meanwhile, Derek and I frantically bailed water, rowed against the winds and swell, fiddled with the hose lines and battery cables, constantly trying to re-start the motor. Finally, Derek says that a set's coming and that we have to abandon ship. In the few seconds available, I unleashed my surfboard from the boat railing, jumped on the surfboard and scratched over the first wave of the set. The 13-foot boat was picked up like a bathtub toy and flipped upside down on the face of the wave in what felt like slow motion. My guess is that the face of the wave was 15 feet plus. The entire boat fit easily inside the wave standing on end. I sat in shock wanting to paddle in to salvage the boat, which looked like a small child in distress. I turned just in time to see the second larger wave of the set towering over me. With a few strong strokes I thought I could punch through the lip of the wave, but it had other plans for me.

I felt myself being sucked over the falls, hanging on tight to the surfboard. On impact, the board was torn from my hands and I was being thrown around in the dark bubbling abyss, not knowing which way was up. Trying to stay relaxed, I finally hit the sandy bottom with my head, turned myself around, and pushed hard off the bottom for the surface. The foam was thick on the surface as I gulped for air, just in time to see the third wave of this set looming overhead. I realized about this time that my surfboard leash was not attached to my ankle, that I was wearing a sweatshirt under a rain jacket, and that my wetsuit was only pulled up to my waist. I was, in effect, a human anchor in the impact zone of huge surf and trying desperately to keep my head above the surface.

Grabbing a big gulp of air, I went under the third wave, then the fourth. I was extremely weak when I saw Derek paddle over to me like an angel from heaven.

On shore, after thanking my lucky stars for surviving, we hustled over to the boat which, because the anchor was out, drifted gently toward the rocks but was spared any significant damage. After righting the boat, we pulled it along the shoreline and up onto the dry sand where the van and trailer could come down and haul it out. Gear was washing up all along the beach and cliffs. An empty gas can was lodged firmly in the rock cliff; clothes, food, and surfing gear were washing in with the waves.

About this time, Jim and Paul drive up with a park ranger and a few other people. Together, we load the boat on the trailer and are at Taco Bell by 4:00 P.M.

We haven't yet had any similar experiences on the kayak trip, fortunately, but there's a long distance still to complete. Large surf is always the greatest fear I have as we kayak south to Mexico.

The color of the ocean today as we paddle to Oceanside Harbor is one of my favorites. It's that dark blue/gray color. The smell of the ocean and its kelp beds, the salty taste in my mouth, and the constant rocking and rolling with the swells heightens one's senses. In the ocean kayak, I am quick to remind myself of our insignificance on this mass of water and yet am impressed with the great beauty she possesses. A sailor must feel this beauty as he or she glides along the surface under the power of the wind. It's an experience that must be felt . . . words can't properly describe the feeling.

We finally turn the corner into the harbor at Oceanside. Protected from the winds and waves now, we can once again make great strides in distance with much less effort. The Oceanside Marina Inn is less than a mile from the harbor mouth and it feels great to take a long hot shower and slip into warm, dry clothes at the hotel. The hotel management allows us to store the kayaks and paddleboards under the hotel in "the dungeon," the 150-

degree boiler room where the naughty guests that steal the wash-cloths are put overnight.

Dinner at the Monterey Bay Cannery is good, and we share good conversation and laughs together. We're all quite tired and are fast asleep by 11:00 P.M.

Next morning, I saunter over to The Jolly Roger Restaurant to check on their opening time. It doesn't open until 7:00 A.M. so I purchase the $2 Sunday newspaper, scamper up the rocks at the harbor, and catch up on the world events. I'm watching the commercial fishing boats head out for the morning, listening to the captain on the loudspeaker announce, "No overhead casting from the boats . . . .in the galley is the beautiful Teresa . . . .we should have a great day fishing . . . ." to the coffee-clutching, Pendleton-clad, overweight men on the stern seeking the elusive big one.

At 9:00 A.M., with full stomachs, we're back on the water and it's already bumpy water. With El Nino in effect, the water temperature is fluctuating between 72 and 74 degrees, unusually warm for this time of year. Dolphins and jellyfish are prevalent as we work our way south.

We paddle hard against the wind-chopped waves for what seems like an eternity at times. Constantly checking our progress by evaluating position to various landmarks on shore, we paddle past Carlsbad, Encinitas, Swami's, and Cardiff.

This section of coastline is known for its excellent surfing, diving, and fishing. But today, with the strong onshore winds and whitecaps, the surf isn't appealing. But it's not hard to imagine what this coastline looks like when a strong south swell is pushing through in glassy conditions.

I haven't spent too much time in these waters but I certainly like the hometown feel of the communities along this coast. Encinitas, Leucadia, and Solana Beach are all very attractive beach towns without that ritzy glamour that Newport and Laguna demonstrate. I suspect if we weren't living in Santa Barbara, Valerie and I would be very comfortable and happy anywhere along this stretch of coast. And I certainly like the feel of the warm water that we're paddling through.

At late afternoon with various families and small groups of friends picnicking on the beach, we paddle in at Del Mar City Beach. The checkered table clothes on the beach, wine, pate and cheese plates remind me of the cover of *Sunset* magazine, or a scene from a Martha Stewart article, quite appealing as we unshaven pirates plod up their beach in search of a fresh water hose bib to rinse the salt water from our bodies.

We talk a homeowner into the use of his garden hose to rinse off and load the gear in and on the van. A quick dinner at Tony Jacal's Mexican restaurant (awesome carnitas burritos) in Solana Beach and we're on our way home.

The fifth leg is complete. Approximately 66 miles were paddled on this leg for a cumulative distance of 288 miles to date, with approximately 56 miles to go to the Mexican border.

LEG SIX

DEL MAR TO MEXICO
OCTOBER 2–5, 1997

CREW: Dave Powdrell, John Beardsmore, Lee Walker, Derek Levy, Mark Levy, Richard Herald, Dave Baxter, Jim Doughty, Doug Powdrell, Tom Powdrell, Earle Powdrell, and Jason Huff

L ogistics get more interesting with 12 paddlers and a 300-mile drive to the starting point. Rather than rent kayaks in Santa Barbara and haul them to San Diego, I find Allen Peuth of Mission Bay Paddle Sports in the yellow pages of a San Diego phone book at our library. Allen has all the kayaks and a trailer to boot. In fact, he lines up our campground at Silver Strand State Beach and is my hero.

The itinerary is set . . . Del Mar City Beach to Mission Bay, Mission Bay to Shelter Island, Shelter Island to Silver Strand State Beach, Silver Strand State Beach to the Mexican border, and the Mexican border back to Imperial Beach for pick up.

News reports in *Time Magazine, Newsweek,* and the local newspapers have been describing problems at the California/Mexico border with pictures of the great wall separating the two countries on the beach.

"California Border Crackdown Heats Up," reads the headline in the July 8, 1997 *Newsweek* magazine. Operation Gatekeeper,

the two-year-old crackdown at the California–Baja California
border, could be a victim of its own success. Border patrols have
been fired upon five times during the past month, and officials
suspect frustrated drug lords and would-be immigrants. Matters
may be even worse than reported. Sources tell *Newsweek* that at
least five other recent incidents have been covered up. "It's a war
zone, nothing less," says patrol agent Joseph Dassaro. The Tex-
Mex border has claimed the most fatalities—a patrol officer in
1996 and a Mexican student last May. But back at Imperial Beach,
south of San Diego, patrols are redoubling their arms and armour.

It may be an interesting horseshoe game that I've got planned
using the border fence as the centerline for the upcoming game.

We leave my house in Santa Barbara at 4:00 A.M. sharp, headed
for Mission Bay where we'll pick up the trailer and six additional
kayaks from Allen at Mission Bay. We arrive at 8:30 A.M., right
on schedule, and hook everything up to the van.

At 9:30 A.M., we pull into Del Mar City Beach and find Earle,
Jason, Doug, Tom, Lee, Doug's wife, Patty, and his daughter, Holly,
all grouped together on the beach. As the van eases to a stop, four
huge set waves slam hard in the outer waters . . . it's a solid six-
foot day with 8–10-foot faces on the sets.

A lifeguard pulls up in his truck and we review our game plan
with him. I'm very concerned about paddling the kayaks through
this surf, especially with rookie paddlers. This is certainly the largest surf we've encountered to date and I'm running worst case
options through my head as another set looms on the horizon.
We all agree that it would be very dangerous attempting to get
kayaks out through these waves. Lifeguard Russ recommends that
we drive the kayaks down a half mile or so to Torrey Pines State
Park or even to La Jolla Cove if it's still too big. I suspect he
doesn't want to deal with rescue attempts this early in the morning. Torrey Pines and La Jolla will be more protected from these
northbound freight train swells.

The large surf we're facing is remnants of Hurricane Pauline
off the Mexican coast. Hurricane Pauline has just killed over 200

impoverished people in Acapulco, Mexico, ravishing their homes and sending people to their death in the huge storm surf. The swells we're facing are being enhanced by two additional storms off the New Zealand coast, Russ informs us. Regardless, we've got huge waves to contend with and, according to all my manuals, large surf is the number one thing to fear when ocean kayaking.

We load everyone up and move down to Torrey Pines State Park where La Jolla Point is protecting the beach. Much more manageable at three to four feet, a few paddlers tumble in the surf before making it out to the open ocean, but it's not life-threatening.

As we start out toward La Jolla Bay, however, it's quickly apparent that the swells are still huge in the outer waters. The recurring thought about how we bring the kayaks to the beach keeps jostling my mind; we'll deal with it as it comes.

An hour into the paddle, we approach La Jolla Cove looking for a safe place to land for lunch, but nothing is available. The waves are crashing hard on the cliff walls and the surf is pummeling all the beaches along the coastline.

I find a small private beach just below the cliffs at La Jolla that has potential as a landing point, but am immediately told by the lifeguard on a bullhorn not to attempt to land. We find out four days later that there have been several deaths at this beach due to the huge surf along the rocks.

We tie up to a lobster buoy 100 yards from shore and hook all the kayaks together. The swells and currents are impressive in their strength. Our viewpoint from the water is excellent, however, as we're able to look south into an awesome reef break. The water color is aquamarine and the waves are spitting. Three surfers are attempting it, but taking a beating on the steep take-offs.

The kayaks constantly bump hard into each other as the swells toss us around. Canned tuna, mayonnaise, pepper sauce, potato chips, and bread are opened and sandwiches made. Jim and John do an excellent job of juggling all of these ingredients and preparing lunch for the crew while being tossed up, down, forward and backward in their kayaks.

Tom, Earle, and Jason look a bit tired but I know they're doing fine. Tom hints that this is harder than he had expected.

I'm so impressed with Tom's joining us on this trip. Tom is one of my younger brothers, who measures 6'3" tall and weighs in at about 235 pounds. Tom's not in the best physical shape having lived the past dozen years in Visalia, the fast-food capital of the world. He has a beautiful wife and newborn baby, Griffin, and he had about a dozen valid excuses available to back out of this trip. But he was adamant about going on this last leg, and, in fact, was instrumental in recruiting our two other brothers in joining us on this leg.

I can tell by the look on his face that he's tired and perhaps a bit leery about his ability to complete this trek. We have all had those same doubts on our first kayak trips. Questions like "Will I be holding everyone else up? What will I do if my arms give out? What options are available if I get too far behind and can't catch up?" pop up about this time.

"Do you need anything, Tom?" is the best that I can muster up.

"No, I'm fine," he responds.

I know that the second day will be easier for him, the third day yet easier, and that he'll be ready to lift a Volkswagen by the end of the fourth day. I truly admire his courage and strength in kayaking these last 56 miles to Mexico with us.

Occasional eight-foot sets break just inside of our kayaks. If a freak set wave would break outside of us, I'm not sure how we'd survive. Bodies, kayaks, and ropes would all be intertwined and thrown around violently. I'm relieved when we finally finish lunch, unhook the kayaks from each other, and resume the paddle south.

Everyone gets settled in to their respective rhythm now as we glide up and down the dark storm swells. Coming around the La Jolla cliffs, we see the long stretch of Mission Beach, looking hard for the Big Dipper ferris wheel off Belmont Park, near our hotel.

When we finally get to the point where we can see our hotel, the intimidating waves bring us to an option: do we paddle directly in to shore and deal with the surf or do we paddle another three miles south into the smooth waters of the Mission Bay jetty to our hotel. I suspect that the tired paddlers will vote for a direct line to the shore and that the veterans will want to paddle around into the harbor. To my pleasant surprise, everyone votes to paddle the extra three miles.

Camping on the beach is fun, but, again, there's nothing quite like a long, hot shower in a clean hotel room after spending the day at sea. We saunter into downtown Mission Bay with the strong scent of aftershave trailing us. A deserted Mexican restaurant on the main drag catches our eye; this is too good to be true. We pig out on awesome carnitas burritos, tacos, taquitos, and chips.

Jason, we discover at dinner, did not apply any sunscreen to his feet. Both feet are swollen with blisters the size of quarters. He hasn't complained a bit, but I know they must be painful.

After the huge dinner, I threaten to take the guys across the street to the Big Dipper and ride nonstop until someone pukes. But my threat becomes muted when I find out that the ride had closed just an hour earlier. Rats.

We saunter back to our rooms and are fast asleep just as *Seinfeld* comes to an end . . . 9:30 P.M. It's been a 19-hour day with a good workout in between.

The next morning I recruit Lee and Dave to help me transport vehicles to Shelter Island, our next stop on the trip to Mexico.

By 7:30 the gang is all together at the Bahia Hotel restaurant eating more than their fill at the buffet. I suspect the hotel accountants who track sales and inventory had to recheck their numbers that afternoon, as we consumed enough food for the entire third floor of the hotel. The journal entries for our breakfast went something like this:

Debit Cash $87.   Credit Sales $87.
Debit Cost of Sales $246.   Credit Inventory $246.
The net effect was a loss of $159 on the income statement.

Other important accounting facts of the case:

Registered Guests: 343

Projected Food Intake: 65 pounds

Actual Food Intake: 121 pounds

Memo to Management: Accountants alert: Assume major pilfering . . . check who worked the morning shift between 7:00 A.M. and 10:00 A.M., October 3.

As we begin our paddle out the Mission Bay harbor mouth, the hurricane swells greet us again. The swell has continued to grow and I'm thankful we don't have to paddle out from the beach as the jetty protects us nicely from any whitewater. However, I'm quick to remember that we'll probably have lunch from the kayaks again and won't be getting out until we reach San Diego Bay, some 12 miles away.

This stretch of coastline along Ocean Beach is lined with 200-foot sandstone cliffs and small pockets of sandy beaches. The morning fog soon lifts and the sky is turning pale blue. Occasionally dolphins and seals are sighted as we meander toward Sunset Cliffs.

The surf at Sunset Cliffs is big and beautiful, and no surfers are in the water. Doug and John decide to unleash Doug's surfboard and trade off catching waves while we watch on the sidelines in the deep water. These six- and seven-foot waves are relatively gentle in the deep water, much like a wave at San Onofre, and before long Richard and Dave decide to try catching a few waves in their kayaks. Richard takes the first crash of the day, but his disabled kayak stops short of the cliffs as he swims in to it. This gives the rest of us the courage to take a few waves ourselves.

Before long we're all hooting and hollering, gliding down these huge waves in kayaks that have zero maneuvering ability. An occasional late take-off ejects the rider from his kayak, requiring a long swim. No significant concern arises for the safety of the kayak, however, as it washes gently into deep water short of the cliffs. For two full hours, we're board surfing and kayak surfing these impressive waves and just loving it.

I have one image in my mind that I will never forget. As a large set approaches, Doug takes off on his surfboard. Nearly double overhead on the takeoff, I see Dave (whose kayak happens to be carrying all our food provisions) also take off on the wave. As they're both zooming down the face of this wave, I see Dave bail out the back of his kayak, fearing a collision with Doug. After bailing out, however, Dave's kayak continues to ride the wave in perfect position with Doug confidently surfing within arm's length of the runaway lunch wagon. His kayak got one of the longest rides of the day, solo.

We finally decide it's time to continue the journey south to San Diego Bay. Tom and Earle have gone on ahead but we hope to catch them before the bay.

The next five miles to Point Loma are owned and maintained by the U.S. military. Occasional jets zoom overhead, helicopters buzz above us, and huge Coast Guard vessels maneuver near us.

Earle and Tom have stopped at the entrance to San Diego Bay amid the amazing air and water show in front of us. All military aircraft had been grounded the two weeks prior due to a number of recent unexplained crashes. The pent-up demand to get airborne was being exhibited today with dozens of fighter jets, helicopters, and other assorted military aircraft flying overhead. I can imagine the fear the residents of Baghdad felt a few years ago with those fighting birds overhead.

Peanut butter and jelly sandwiches are prepared at a small beach just inside San Diego Bay, protected from any significant surf. A few of the guys trade off surfing at Point Loma, which is breaking about two feet. The hot sun feels good as we sprawl out on the beach and sit among the rocks, not unlike seals and sea lions we've seen along the coast. We can see Mexico for the first time now, as we peer 12 miles down the coastline. For the first time, I can sense the completion of this adventure, and it is with mixed emotions.

As we pack up the gear and begin paddling into San Diego Bay, we're greeted with a menagerie of visual and audio stimulation. Some of the docks are packed tight with Brandt's cormorants, the blackbirds that typically gather and feed in flocks of several hundred at a time. When they feed, the cormorants swim down below the surface in unison, acting much like a huge fishing net. The shallow swimming fish have little refuge.

Seals are swimming around the docks barking loudly at the cormorants. The robust brown pelicans, some measuring four feet tall, are outnumbered, but sit perched with their sophisticated, all-knowing attitude. A California sea lion, with his high fore-head, is arguing with somebody about something. His bark is significantly louder and threatening and his size, perhaps seven feet in length, is impressive. I paddle slightly away from him, hoping he's not pissed off at me.

Some of the seals are swimming along with us, occasionally bobbing their heads near our bows. These are the moments that make kayaking the coastline most memorable to me, being among the wildlife in their natural habitat.

Equally impressive are the submarines, aircraft carriers, and other naval ships in the bay. These floating cities are truly engineering masterpieces. We paddle up and touch a few of them before we're told to stay 500 feet clear of all ships.

When we eventually arrive at our hotel dock, Dennis Connor's Stars and Stripes catamaran is parked at the dock. We take a group picture next to it before being greeted by Derek and Mark, who have paddled their paddleboards from Del Mar to Mission Bay, then driven their car down to paddle the rest of the trip with us.

Derek, Mark, and I drive back up to Mission Bay to pick up cars and transport them south to Imperial Beach at the YMCA Surf Camp, where we'll spend the next night. By the time we get back to Shelter Island, about two hours later, it's dark and we're all hungry. It is at this time that I discover that Earle, Tom, and Doug have their gear in Tom's car, which is also down at Imperial Beach now. So they have nothing but the wet clothes on their backs. The thought of driving to Imperial Beach and back is a nightmare to me and the guys heroically slip into some other dry clothes for the evening.

Dave Baxter used to live near San Diego and introduces us to the Boll Weevil Restaurant. Humungous hamburgers, pitchers of beer, and two pool tables keep us occupied. Two young girls whipping us at the pool table provide good laughs until we make our way home at 10:30.

After a big birthday breakfast for Jason the next morning, complete with singing cooks, waiters, and fellow hotel patrons, we gear up for the paddle down San Diego Bay.

With the tide coming up, we'll be getting the benefit of water coming into the bay. At 11:30 A.M., however, the tide turns, which can be equivalent to paddling upstream a three-mile-per-hour river given proper tide conditions.

Under glassy conditions, we paddle south past the beautiful luxury boats in San Diego Bay. Dozens upon dozens of massive naval ships and submarines also line the bay.

A quick pit stop at the Hotel Del Coronado to stretch our legs, we admire the wealthy people in their suits promenading on the fresh-cut lawns sipping coffee while they delight in our disheveled, adventurous appearance.

It's good to be with Derek and Mark again. Their energy brings new life to the conversation base, which is always good. Tom, Earle, and Jason don't know Derek and Mark, and I'm glad they get the chance to talk.

After four hours of paddling down the bay, we're at Silver Strand State Beach Park, where we'll take the kayaks out of the water, then hike them through a 200-yard tunnel that takes us back to the Pacific Ocean. The gnarly surf reacquaints itself to us as we exit the tunnel and stare out to the coastline again.

Two marines are paddling a tandem kayak in and out of the surf, which gives us some perspective on the size and intensity of the surf. They get pounded hard several times, but eventually make it out into the deep water.

After lunch at the picnic tables at Silver Strand, we batten down the hatches of the kayaks, tie everything down that might wash away in the surf, and begin the arduous process of paddling through the huge shore break. Derek and Mark are a huge help to most everyone as they march the kayaks into deep water and hold the paddlers steady until the lull appears. Then they give the shove that helps get the momentum up.

Richard paddles up the face of one wave just as the wave is about to crest. His kayak dances a jig on its tail on the backside of the wave before he fortunately falls forward and continues the paddle to deep water.

Jason is less fortunate as a set wave pummels him. The wave ends up folding his kayak in half, filling the hull entirely with water. Not a great experience for someone from Texas used to dealing with significantly milder surf conditions.

Jason was on his high school swim team and is a former marine. But right now he looks more like a boxer who lost a bout with Mike Tyson. His knees are a little weak and there may be a few stars dancing in his view.

After recomposing himself and with Derek's encouragement, he is launched again from shore and makes it out safely. John and I go last and both take a beating. My kayak is folded in half after I bail out at the last minute of a set wave. John gets worked on several sets before making it out safely.

Eventually, we all survive the ordeal and are thankful to be out. At this point, I'm thinking that we might want to change plans slightly . . . perhaps we paddle directly to Mexico now, then paddle back up to Imperial Beach. This course of action would mean having to deal with the shore break only once more, rather than three more times. But consensus among the troops is to stick to the original plan.

After paddling the three miles to Imperial Beach, we're met by Tristen on a jet ski. Tristen is a young bloke from Australia who is one of the lifeguards at the YMCA Camp Surf. He directs us where to paddle in for our stay at their campgrounds.

Camp Surf is a little known enclave in Imperial Beach that is available by reservation only to large groups of children, typically Boy Scouts and Girl Scouts. It includes an archery range, a skateboard park, a ropes course, horseshoe pits, a theater stage, as well as two miles of private beach to swim and learn to surf. We stumbled upon the camp from fellow kayaker Allen Peuth who indicated that the camp directors occasionally accept overnight kayakers.

We set up camp as far as possible from the 200 Girl Scouts who had reserved the facility. There, we dig our fire pit, set up the poker /

dining table from a piece of drift plywood, and get the bar-b-ques fired up.

The appetizer is menudo, the Mexican soup made of the cow parts that nobody else can eat (a reminder of an old surf trip to Mexico we took years ago). The main course is salmon, lobster, and steak burritos and tropical fruit in light syrup. For dessert, we have the pleasure of Loy Beardsmore's famous triple chocolate brownies smothered in chewy caramel.

After gorging ourselves, we break out the poker gear and automatic card shuffler. You can only buy chips with something other than money. Hats, T-shirts, pocketknives, a pair of sweatpants, and sunglasses come across the table and are exchanged for equal value poker money. After hours of play, the players are whittled down to Lee, Dave, Derek, and Richard. Lee ends up taking the pot of clothing and paraphernalia. I suspect he's donated most of it to Goodwill by now and will deduct it on his tax return as a charitable contribution.

The surf during the night is very loud and the beach vibrates slightly as the sets hit hard. But the stars are out and it is warm.

The next morning after a light breakfast and coffee and some talk around the campfire, we hit the shore break with a vengeance. I decide to face it first and, after waiting for the lull, charge at it with everything I have. Miraculously, I didn't get my hair wet, a first for me. Jim follows just behind me and gets totally worked, losing his kayak and having to swim in. John has a few mishaps, but Earle and Tom make it out without any difficulty. Jason takes his lumps again, however. He gets pounded hard by another two sets and is completely exhausted when Derek gets to him. Wanting to throw in the towel and wait on the beach for our return, Derek sits him down and together, they decide to take one more shot at it. Lee swims in with the thought of paddling Jason's kayak out and having Jason swim out past the breakers. But as Lee is paddling in, Jason is paddling out in his kayak with the look of a madman on his face. He makes it safely to deep water and we are happy he is with us for the final day.

Imperial Beach looks much like Hermosa Beach or Manhattan Beach did ten years ago; small beach cottages on the sand next to an occasional beach mansion. After Imperial Beach, however, the coastline is deserted to the Mexican border. No signs of military police or border agents, only occasional sightings of fishermen casting effortlessly into the surf.

Tijuana Sloughs, a famous surfing spot, is breaking with seven-foot waves. A few off-the-wall surfers are screaming and laughing at each other and having a comical surf session. None of us catch any waves there before continuing to Mexico, hoping to catch a few on the way back.

Before long, the bullring at Tijuana is in sight; then the great wall that separates our countries. As we're making our way closer to the border, I'm paddling by myself and am getting teary-eyed. I reflect briefly on the 19 days that we've paddled, the laughter we've shared, and the sights we've seen. I'm sad that this adventure is ending.

The houses in Mexico are a sharp contrast to the beach houses of America. Ours are gray and white; theirs are pink and green. Ours appear neat and orderly lined up on the sand; theirs are more randomly spread on the hillside. Our streets are freshly paved; theirs are dirt roads. And yet I have as much appreciation for the Mexican lifestyle and its people as I do for our own. In many respects, it's even more appealing.

We reach the border wall in unison and raise our paddles together as we drift into Mexican water. Nobody from either nation is on the beach to congratulate us, but nobody is there to shoot at us either. We have paddled 56 miles in kayaks that some long-distance kayak aficionados refer to as tricycles, and it feels exhilarating.

The surf continues to pummel the coastline hard. Wouldn't it be a fine finish if one of us got caught inside and hauled onto the Mexican beach without a passport, I'm pondering? I'm glad when we start paddling back toward Imperial Beach where our cars are parked, immediately feeling the wind at our faces. It will be a slower journey back, but fortunately, not a long one.

Mark Levy has paddled hard and fast and is the first one to arrive back at Tijuana Sloughs. A set wave approaches and I see him paddle hard for the wave. As he catches it, I see that this wave is gigantic. He is dwarfed by the whitewater; in fact I lose sight of him as the wave fully engulfs him and his 16-foot paddleboard. I can't see him until some 50 yards later, when he pulls out of the wave.

John Beardsmore lines up for an equally large set wave, but the wave breaks directly behind him and he's catapulted out of his kayak. Derek catches that last wave at Tijuana Sloughs, a big left, before we work our way back to the YMCA Camp Surf.

Derek and I arrive at the campground first and we each catch decent-sized waves to the shore, but without incident. But the next half hour turns out to be the scariest of the trip for me. Earle, Jason, and Tom are paddling in the deep water waiting for a lull before paddling in to the beach. For some reason, the sets are relentless right now as they sit and wait outside the breakers.

Suddenly Derek and I see a rogue set coming. Tom and Jason, whose kayaks are pointed toward shore, stroke their kayaks in reverse and just make it over the first of four waves, each with a face of ten feet. But Earle is slightly inside of them and unable to get his kayak over the set wave. I see him bail out of the kayak just as the impact of the wave hits the kayak. His kayak comes washing in, folded in half, but I don't see Earle anywhere. I know he has a red life vest on, so he should be easy to spot, but still no sign of him after the second, then third set waves break. Both Derek and I are running in the water now looking hard for him to pop up. Just before the fourth wave breaks, his head pops up, eyes round like saucers. He gives us the thumbs up, thank God, and swims in to shore smiling.

Earle is a great athlete and competitor, but like Jason, without much experience in large surf. He didn't surf with us in high school and, once he moved to Texas to work with NASA on the Space Shuttle, has spent little time in the ocean. But he proved to be the hero of the trip, in my mind, staying calm in an extremely dangerous situation. The life vest proved to be both a help and a hindrance in the large surf. Because of its flotation, Earle wasn't able to dive below the impact of these huge waves. He had to take it head on, directly at the ocean's surface. On the other hand, and more importantly, the life vest kept his head above water between waves, and I'm thankful he had it on. I think I heard him yell, "Houston, we have a problem!!" just before the first wave broke on him.

Tom and Jason eventually get the O.K. sign from Derek that we're in a lull and they paddle like banshees to the beach. Both get tossed out of their kayaks from the next waves, but it's not a threatening situation. Doug, Mark, Richard, Dave, and Jim come in later, again without incident. The journey is over.

As we're packing gear and kayaks in the vehicles, my wife, Valerie, Loy Beardsmore, and Janice Baxter come screeching up the dirt road with champagne bottles flowing. They've flown down from Santa Barbara to congratulate us and it's great to see them.

Dinner at the Chart House at La Jolla was excellent that evening. After dessert, we pop open a couple of piñatas that Derek and I had made up, Derek's in the shape of California, mine in the shape of a kayak (neither of us knew the other had made a piñata).

On the six-hour drive back to Santa Barbara, as I see various exit signs on the freeway, I reflect back on events and feelings I had during that portion of the kayak trip. I'm truly thankful for what we were able to experience along this southern third of California coastline. And more importantly than the experience of paddling was the thankfulness for having such great friends. As my brother, Tom, put it afterwards, all the money in the world is meaningless compared to having great friends. Clearly, these are the best kinds of friends.

The future of kayaking along the California coast looks very promising. Kayak trails along various sections of the coast and among the neighboring islands are being considered as I write this journal. I will strongly encourage these kayak trails and hope that kayak camping accommodations are made available from the Oregon border to Mexico. I also hope that by kayaking, more people become aware of the fragile nature of the California coastline. The American Oceans Campaign and Surfrider Foundation actively work to protect these waters for future generations. Get involved with them.

It's nice to know that we've completed the journey and I hope that others will take on similar challenges in life. There are so many wonderful things to see and do and as long as we have our health, I'll continue to look for unusual experiences to take with my friends and family.

FINAL STATISTICS OF THE JOURNEY:

Total days paddled:	19
Total miles paddled:	344
Average miles per day paddled:	18.11
Longest one-day paddle (in miles):	26
Approximate total paddle strokes:	344,000
Approximate calories burned:	51,600

REFERENCES

Broze, Matt C., and George Gronseth. *Sea Kayaker's Deep Trouble: Ture Stories and Their Lessons from Sea Kayaker Magazine*.

California Coastal Commission. *California Coastal Access Guide*, 4th edition.

Chesnut, Merlyn. *The Gaviota Land*.

Dowd, John. *Sea Kayaking: A Manual for Long Distance Touring*, 3rd edition.

Hollister-Wheelwright, Jane. *The Ranch Papers*.

McConnaughey, Bayard H., and Evelyn McConnaughey. *The Pacific Coast*.

Romana-Lax, Andromeda. *Sea Kayaking in Baja*.

Tompkins, Walker A. *Goleta the Good Land and Rancho Royale*.

American Oceans Campaign
725 Arizona Avenue, Suite 102
Santa Monica, CA 90401
(310) 576-6162
fax (310) 576-6170
www.americanoceans.org

Surfrider Foundation USA
122 S. El Camino Real #67
San Clemente, CA 92672
(714) 492-8170
fax (714) 492-8142
www.surfrider.org/

ABOUT THE AUTHOR

D avid Powdrell moved to Palos Verdes, California, on the Southern California coastline as a wide-eyed teenager from the hot, dry climate of Carson City, Nevada, in the summer of 1969. He and his three brothers immediately took to the ocean when the surfing bug bit them. With newly acquired driver's licenses and a van, they took to exploring new surfing locations up and down the California coast.

In the early 1980's, while living in Manhattan Beach, David met the locals of 1st Street, a hilarious group of outstanding surfers and watermen. Together, they made dozens of treks down the rugged dirt roads of Baja, Mexico, up to the frigid waters of San Simeon on California's central coast, in search of fun, uncrowded surf.

David was prompted to write this book for several reasons: to record some of the adventures these best friends have been on together, to record the current status of the ever-changing Southern California coastline, and as an incentive for other "common men" to take on an adventure, in kayak, or otherwise.